CONTINUITY AND CHANGE IN A LITTLE COMMUNITY

A Study of the Bharias of Patalkot in Madhya Pradesh

A.M. KURUP

CONCEPT PUBLISHING COMPANY, NEW DELHI

First Published 1986

Ayyappan Madhava Kurup (*b.* 1929-)

Published by
Naurang Rai
Concept Publishing Company
H-13, Bali Nagar
NEW DELHI-110015 (India)

Printed in India by
Bharat Enterprises
at Chetna Printers
Mauzpur Shahdara Delhi-11053

FOREWORD

MAN SPENDS his life time understanding himself, his family his neighbourhood, his fellow citizens and the world at large in order to live a harmonious existence in a society of man. But a scientific study of human evolution and culture, is only about one-and-a-quarter century old. Anthropologists the world over pursue the study of man from various angles, using different tools and techniques, ideas and concepts, and all the derivative knowledge is put to use in the service of man. In this effort Anthropology has always kept its windows open not only to welcome specialised knowledge but also to recognise the relevance of new specialities, new techniques, tools, concepts and so on like the "law of uniformity" from geology to a Freudian model, or a carbon-fourteen dating from chemistry.

This attempt of Dr Kurup is to empirically test the significance of the statistical method in gauging the rate of change of a geographically isolated tribal group, the Bharia of Patalkot in the State of Madhya Pradesh. The conclusions drawn, in a large measure, prove the utility of statistics in studies on cultural dynamics. The study would, therefore, I am sure stimulate interest leading to further refinement in concepts and techniques.

The analysis of data, their logical interpretation and coherent presentation are an eloquent testimony to the author's long practical experience in tribal development and continued academic interest.

Happy I am to commend the volume to academics, researchers and practitioners.

L.P. VIDYARTHI

Ranchi
1 July 1985

ACKNOWLEDGEMENTS

THE SEEDS of this study were sown in me in the summer of 1960 when, as a teacher in the Tribal Workers' Training Institute, Chhindwara, Madhya Pradesh, I led a group of Indian Administrative/Police Service probationers to Patalkot for a field visit as part of their training programme. Subsequently, I visited the area quite often and continued to acquaint myself with the Bharias of Patalkot. Information gathered during these visits forms the basis of this volume.

But, without the whole hearted co-operation extended by the Bharias, individually and collectively, and their warmth and cordiality, I could not have accomplished this onerous task. To them, I am ever grateful.

The idea of utilising the many important patches of information gathered from Patalkot over the years for a Doctoral thesis was instilled in me by Prof. L.P. Vidyarthi of Ranchi University in 1973, who also cheerfully accepted to guide me. It was also he who persuaded me to revise the material and present it to the readers. I offer my sincere thanks to him for steering me to a successful culmination.

My professional friends and colleagues extended continuous encouragement and helped with suggestions and comments. My thanks to them, in particular to Dr. B. N. Sahay and Dr. Sunil Misra.

Final touches to the dissertation were given in 1978 at the Project Planning Centre, University of Bradford, U.K., where I was pursuing a course in Project Planning as a Colombo Plan

Fellow. Here I had the privilege of exchanging ideas with the Faculty members of the Centre.

Sumam Kurup, my wife, has been a constant inspiration for me; she has also helped in correcting proofs. My special thanks are due to her.

A.M. KURUP

CONTENTS

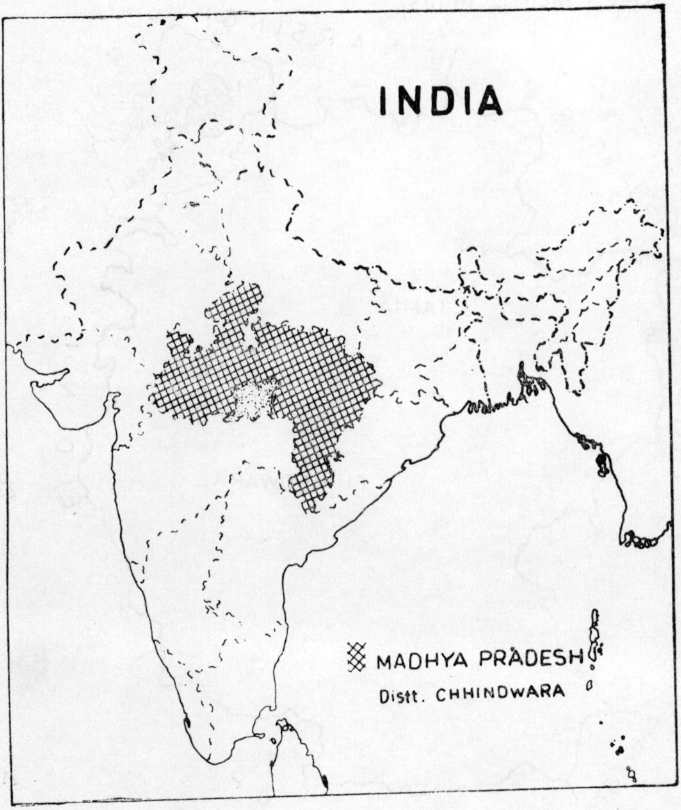
INDIA
MADHYA PRADESH
Distt. CHHINDWARA

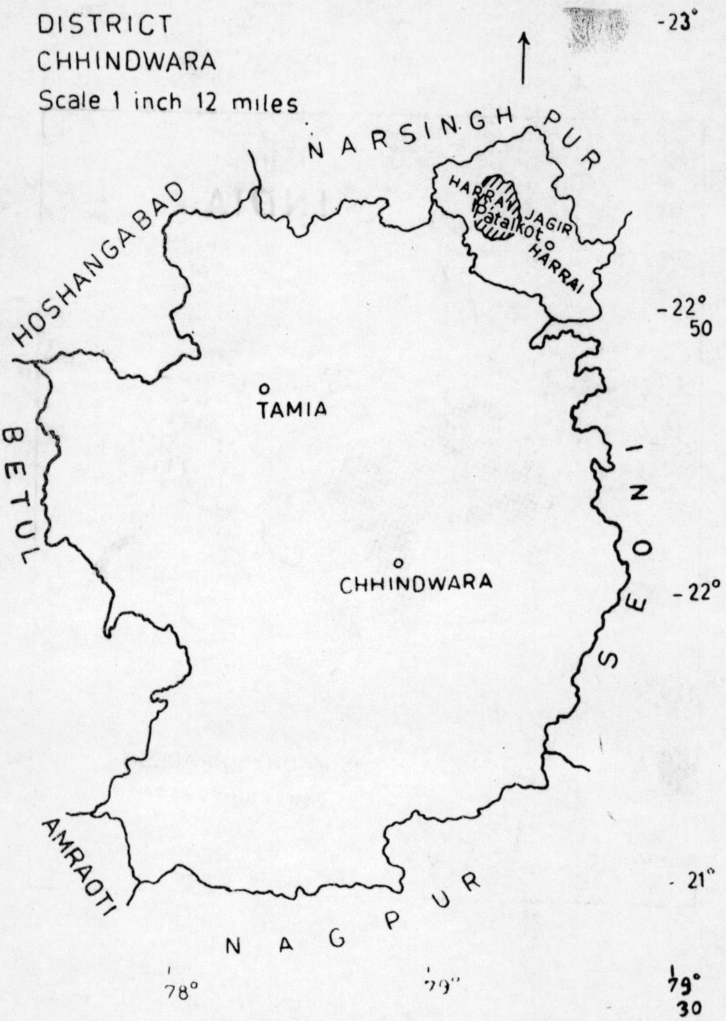
DISTRICT
CHHINDWARA
Scale 1 inch 12 miles
NARSINGH PUR
HOSHANGABAD
HARRAI JAGIR
Patalkot
HARRAI
TAMIA
BETUL
CHHINDWARA
SEONI
AMRAOTI
NAGPUR
-23°
-22° 50
-22°
-21°
78°
79°
79° 30

PROLOGUE

THE CHARACTERISTICS of "a little community" are portrayed in Robert Redfield's[1] *View-points for the Study of a Human Whole.* According to him A Little Community has "the quality of distinctiveness: where the Community begins and where it ends is apparent"; it is small: "it is so small that either it itself is the unit of personal observation or else, being somewhat larger and yet homogeneous, it provides in some part of it a unit of personal observation fully representative of the whole"; it is homogeneous: for, "activities and states of mind are much alike for all persons in corresponding sex and age positions"; and it is self-sufficient: as, "it provides for all or most of the activities and needs of the people in it."[2]

For long, little communities have been the focus of study for anthropologists. They have been studied from various angles by different social scientists. Chang Kom, *A Maya Village* (1934), *The Folk Culture of Yucatan* (1941), *A Village that chose progress* (1950) by Redfield, *The Small Community* (1942) by Morgan, *We, The Tikopia* (1936) by Raymond Firth, *The Nuer* (1940) by Evans Pritchard: *The Affairs of a Tribe* (1950) by Majumdar, *The Kamar* (1951) by Dube; and *The Maler* (1963) by Vidyarthi are a few examples. Models of these studies vary from theoretical/conceptual to empirical, and a combination of both based on an ethnographic/monographic account to higher levels of abstractions and generalisations.

The studies of "Little Communities" have been attempted with a variety of approaches. They range from descriptive accounts of the institutions of the community to cultural dynamics. Studies on the dynamics of culture have generally been undertaken on the basis of "age-area hypothesis", "bench-mark survey" and "available literature" or a combination of them. Restudy of the same community by the same or different authors, over a period of time, has also formed the basis of studies on "culture-dynamics".

The present work is the outcome of a longitudinal study in the "culture dynamics" of a little community of Madhya Pradesh, the "Bharias of Patalkot". The period extends to nearly 30 years. The objective was to comprehend the dynamics of change under the impact of external forces and the efforts for planned development or induced change. This community is unique as far as the habitat is concerned. Surrounded by lofty hills, the area is almost insulated and its interaction with the outside world has been limited and controlled.

The overall objective of the present study was to comprehend the changes that are taking place in the various spheres of life of the Bharias—material, social, economic, ritual and religious—as a sequal to their limited contact with the outside world, particularly in the light of the efforts made by the welfare administration. Implicit in it is an assessment of the life of the Bharias vis-a-vis their physical environment; the dynamics of change taking place in the various institutions of the community; the various forces/agencies responsible for change; the rate and direction of change in relation to the various social institutions; and the factors which accelerate or impede change.

Methodology

It was only at the turn of this century that greater attention was paid to the study of culture change among the primitive communities. The purpose varied from academic interest in tracing the course of development of human society to administrative action to find out the impact of welfare measures. In India, studies in culture change are mainly viewed as a body of knowledge aimed at providing leads for administrative action. Several extensive researches or fact-finding surveys have been undertaken to find out the social and economic changes taking place in the village communities, caste groups and tribal societies. A number of such studies were conducted during the decade and a half after Independence, particular emphasis being on the study of change after the abolition of Zamindari and inception of the community development programme.

Most of these studies attempted to explain, in qualitative terms, the trend of changes discernible in the community. A common approach adopted in such studies was to compare two situations at two different points of time on the basis of what was given in literature and what was observed by the researcher. This method has its limitations so much so that the exact change or persistence of a particular custom or behaviour was often lost sight of.

The present study is so designed that within the general framework of the methods like observation (both participant and non-participant), group discussions and interviews (using schedules) an element of quantification has also been introduced. This was basically to understand the changes that are taking place in the various spheres of life of the tribe as a sequel to their limited contact with the outside world on the one hand and the efforts made by the welfare administration on the other. Emphasis, therefore, has been given to the genealogical techniques of study. This method is adopted because of two important limitations, namely, micro vs. macro change and macro change involving nearly a generation. No authentic descriptive information on the Bharias of Patalkot is available so as to make use of the same as bench-mark data. Moreover, their habitat is such that practically no one is intimately aware of the past socio-cultural life of the people. The only recourse, therefore, was to collect information on their past culture from the informants. This method obviously was fraught with the danger of "memory lapse". To obviate this to the extent possible, it was decided to select only a few definable customs and practices (culture traits) covering a broad spectrum of Bharia culture and also those which could easily be remembered by the informants. For the purpose of convenience each definable custom or practice was considered as one trait.[3] Thus, use of a particular dress or a hair style, the custom of payment of bride price, the occasions when the services of the magician were made use of, etc., were taken as traits. In other words "trait analysis", in the broader sense, was adopted as the research technique in this study.

Making allowance for any memory lapse every care was taken to reduce it to the minimum. Information was checked and cross-checked with different members of the family and even neighbours both individually and collectively. It is well-known that some aspects of culture change more rapidly than others. For example, the food habits of a community may change faster with the introduction of a new crop in the area than the method of selection of spouse. Constant contact with the local market (where different groups of people assemble) may bring in change in the pattern of dress more rapidly when compared to the worship of a regional deity. In other words changes in culture traits could be the result of various factors, important being contact and communication. However, changes which do not alter the social structure of a community are accepted more rapidly.

The culture of the Bharias of Patalkot is largely conditioned by their physical environment. Although the neighbouring people live not far away from them, their interaction is controlled, to a large extent, by geographical barriers. The high mountains all around the Patalkot valley prevent outsiders from making free contact with the Bharias. Under pressing circumstances, however, the Bharias do make limited visits outside the valley, either to the weekly market or to the nearest government office. The communication or interaction between the Bharias and the outside people, therefore, is limited and controlled. This being so, it was decided to select a few broad areas of the Bharia culture, covering a wide spectrum of their customs, manners, economy, etc., for a close scrutiny. These were material culture, economic, social and religious life, and leadership. While selecting the broader areas of Bharia culture, the guiding factor was the behaviour of culture traits towards external forces. The study included: (i) peripheral culture traits which could be easily amenable to change due to culture contacts and other external influences like material culture; (ii) core culture traits which were not easily amenable to change either by contact or other forces, like religious life; and (iii) culture traits which fall in between the above two, like the social life, which take various shades of change under the influence of contact and other external forces.

The study of the life and culture of the Bharias of Patalkot, in general, was supplemented by case studies of 24 families. This helped in understanding more closely the behaviour pattern of culture traits.

Patalkot valley has 13 villages inhabited by 91 households of Bharias and 21 households of Gonds. Being a closed community the different villages in the valley provided close cultural homogeneity. The case studies were conducted in two of the villages.

Reference period

The present study covers a period of nearly three decades. Any scientific inquiry relating to the assessment of change in culture over a period of time necessitates selection of two definite periods, one representing the past and the other the present. In choosing the past it was ensured that the time difference was long enough to perceive changes. To minimise "memory lapse" a landmark in the life of the people was chosen for easy recall. Generally speaking, it was assumed that the informants were more likely to remember some happening which took place at a critical time or period of their life.

In the case of this study 1945 was taken as the "past reference period" and 1975 as the "present period". Thus, a 30 year gap was considered "enough time" to notice change in a given culture. The reasons for selection of 1945 as the bench-mark period were threefold. First, it represented the "Zamindari" period when the Bharias lived at the mercy of the local chieftains who were more interested in their personal gain than in the welfare of the people. In fact, this period refers to a time when the people had no state-controlled welfare activities. Secondly, 1945 represented the period just after the Second World War which, to the people of the British territories, remained a landmark in their life. This was also the time when the freedom movement for India's Independence almost reached a turning point. To the Bharias of Patalkot, however, 1945 represented a period of a tragic event, when a huge landslide took place resulting in the death of many people and devastation of their agricultural fields. In fact, this particular event, in most of the cases, helped in pinpointing the time and minimising recall lapse.

Collection of data

Collection of data for this study covered a span of more than 15 years. I have been in touch with the Bharias of Patalkot for nearly two decades beginning with 1958. It was in 1958 also that the first ever systematic benchmark survey was undertaken by the Tribal Research Institute in Chhindwara, Madhya Pradesh, where I was an official. Subsequent visits took place in 1961, 1972 and 1976. The 1976 visit mainly helped in clarifying a few points. These visits gave me an ample opportunity to have a close look at the community, their culture and the pace of change that was taking place in the cultural fabric of the community. Before embarking on the field investigations, available published information on the habitat, history and culture of the Bharias was thoroughly consulted. Although some useful information was available on the Bharia tribe of Chhindwara and Jabalpur districts, no documents covered the Bharias of Patalkot. As such, for all practical purposes, Bharias are a less known "little community".

The guiding factor in eliciting various types of information from the individual households was to see that such data reflected the norms of behaviour of the household. Wherever possible, the head of the household was taken as the main informant. However, care was taken to see that the information was cross-checked with other members of the household as well.

A word about the information itself may be necessary at this stage. The Bharia tribe of Patalkot has been leading almost a secluded life, insulated from the main-stream of national life. They had developed a sense of caution and fright in dealing with the outsiders. More particularly when dealing with officials whom they are scared of. I had, therefore, to establish my credentials and rapport with utmost care and caution. Further, the wide information elicited from them required, on their part, consistent thinking and cogency. Utmost care was, therefore, taken in collecting information from the informants.

Analysis of data

Analysis of the data was undertaken in two phases. The first comprised the general descriptive ethnography of the tribe, both past and present, covering aspects like history, physical surroundings, social organisation, leadership, material culture, economic life, and religious life. The second consisted of the analysis of the data collected in the "design sheets". Each design sheet contained information on individual culture traits of 24 households in respect of two periods of time, 1940's and 1970's. The contents of the design sheet were transferred on to a tabulation plan. Individual traits, for the same reference period and for all the households, were put on one sheet.

Finally, an abstract table was prepared containing the typology of the trait on the one side and the incidence of the practice of the same for two different periods of time on the other. This abstract table was analysed, correlated and contrasted to indicate in quantitative terms the incidence of the practice of each culture traits in the two periods. General conclusions are drawn by correlating the dynamics of various culture traits.

REFERENCES

1. Robert Redfield, *The Little Community: View-points for the Study of a Human Whole*, the University of Chicago Press, Chicago and London (seventh impression).
2. Ibid., p. 4.
3. Culture trait has been defined differently by various social scientists. There is a difference even in British and American schools. Kroeber uses the term "culture trait" for the finest element of culture. For purposes of this study "trait" is taken to mean a group of definable and identifiable culture elements to represent a meaningful unit of an aspect of culture.

1

THE SETTING

THE NORTHERN part of Chhindwara district of Madhya Pradesh is a stretch of wild and mountainous country formed by the Satpura range, which rises from the central level of the plateau to the highest elevation and falls again on the north to the Narmada valley. "The long stretch which extends along this crest from east to west may, by courtesy, be called a plateau, but it is really a series of plateaus separated by valleys and ravines."[1] It is almost in the heart of this hilly tract that Patalkot, the "bowl-shaped" valley, the home of the Bharia tribe, is situated.

Patalkot, situated approximately between 22° 24′ and 22° 26′ North, and between 78° 40′ and 79° 10′ East,[2] is about 31 sq miles in area. The valley is hemmed in by Maikal ranges of the Satpuras which have their own local names. On the east of Patalkot is the Motur range; on the south-east, it is flanked by Kabahad, on the north-west the range continues beyond Lotia and Batkakhapa and is called Dulahadev mountain. The hills around the Patalkot valley rise to about 3,300 ft. But the valley itself is about 1,500 ft. below the general elevation and is deeper when it falls to river-beds.[3]

The hills of the southern rim of the valley are steep, showing bare rocks with sheer cliffs. There is little vegetation on these compared to the hills lying on the opposite side which have rather gentle slopes and are covered with thick forests. The slopes of these hills are subject to heavy landslides, capable of demolishing cultivable land. Within the valley the terrain is very uneven. The valleys of Doodhi and its tributary Gaini are deep cut and huge walls of solid granite stand on either side of these rivers. Several streams flowing through the Patalkot and finding their way to Doodhi have also deep-cut valleys. The river and stream beds are often narrow and with banks of sand. The hillocks within the Patalkot area are undulating in character and hold rich forests. But patches of level land are cultivated and used for constructing houses. The entire valley is strewn with boulders and stones.

The rivers

The general slope of the Satpuras is north-to-south so that in Chhindwara district such rivers as Pench and Kanhan which take their origin in the northern ranges flow towards south. But certain rivers such as Denwan and Sitarewa, which originate in the neighbourhood of Patalkot, flow towards the north. The important river of Patalkot is, however, the Doodhi which originates from the southern flank of Patalkot, flows due north and finally joins the Narmada. The Doodhi within the Patalkot itself, is joined by a small stream called Gaini. This stream joins the Doodhi river near village Dudhipatha.

Climate and rainfall

The valley being situated in the Satpuras, the climate of Patalkot is pleasant and wholesome. During summer, the maximum temperature does not exceed 105°F, but during winter, it comes down to about 45°F. Winters are marked with fog and an occasional frost. The Satpuras receive a fairly heavy rainfall ranging between 45 and 60 inches. No separate records exist for Patalkot. However, it has been estimated that the valley receives an annual rainfall of 50 to 60 inches. Most of it is received during the monsoon months between the beginning of July and the end of September. The climate which is bracing and healthy shows a marked influence on the inhabitants of the valley.

The soil

"On the crystalline and Gondwana formations", says Montgomerie[4] describing the soils of this region, "the subsoil is usually sandy and tends to hold up water. At the other end of the scale are the hillsides and slopes on which the gradual decomposition of the rock forms the trap, a thin red soil, and from the crystalline rock a thin yellow soil constantly liable to be swept away by the rush of rain or the sweep of wind." Within the valley two types of soils are found: First, the thinnest, called *barra* and the second, somewhat superior red or yellow, which tends to a brownish colour, called *mutbarra.* Needless to mention that both kinds of soils are poor compared to the deep black soils found in the plains of Chhaurai, south of the plateau. These soils are, however, good for growing small millets like *kodon* and *kutki*, the main crops of the Bharias.

The geology

Chhindwara district is covered by the Deccan trap in which fossiliferous intertrappean sedimentary strata are met with at various localities. There are also considerable expanses of the metamorphic and Gondwana rocks. Patalkot valley as well as the surrounding region comprises Gondwana rocks of the *Mahadeo* series which Montgomerie[5] describes as follows:

"The *Mahadeo* series of upper Gondwana rocks is so named from the Pachmarhi range which is composed of this formation. The *Mahadeo* rocks consist chiefly of very thick massive beds of coarse sandstone, grit and conglomerate. They are frequently ferruginous or marked with ferruginous bands. They are associated with clay and occasionally with bands of impure earthly limestones. The sandstones form high ranges of hills and often weather into vertical scarps of great height, forming conspicuous cliffs in the forest, and contrasting strongly with the black precipices of the Deccan traps and the rounded irregular masses of the more graitoid detamorphic rocks. In the typical area of the Satpura region the *Mahadeo* rocks attain a thickness of at least 10,000 ft. nine-tenths of which consists of coarse sandstone, grit and conglomerate."

The flora

In Patalkot the wide stretches of green forests the exploitation of which began 10 years ago yield to the government substantial revenue. Among the timber trees growing in Patalkot the most important are the *sal* (*Shorea robusta*) which, in commercial importance, is reckoned next to teak, and the *Tinsa* (*ougeinia dalbergioides*). Other trees are the *Haldu* (*Adina cordifolia*), a tall and beautiful tree, and the *lendia* (*lagerstroemia*). In bloom it is covered with clusters of small white sweet-scented flowers. The *saj* (*Terminalia tomentosa*), which grows on the abandoned *dahiya* clearings as well as in the forests, is another important timber tree. The tree is considered sacred by the Gonds and Bharias alike and may not ordinarily be felled by them. The *saj* is a large tree with long, thin, nearly glabrous leaves. Other trees are the *salai* (*Boswellia scrrata*) which may grow straight up 50 to 60 ft., and the *Tendu* [*Diospyrous tomentosa* (the *tendu* leaves are used for making *binri*—handmade cigar)] the fruit of which are consumed. The trees which offer the Bharias minor forest produce are the *harra* (*Terminalia chebula*) which is noticeable for its pale green foliage in the month of April and the *achar* (*Buchanania latifolia*) which yields small juicy fruits and the nuts of which are dried and broken to yield *chirongi*. *Awala* (*Phyllanthus emblica*) trees are also found in plenty. There are a large number of *mahua* trees in Patalkot and the Bharias labour hard to collect the *mahua* flowers for food and for brewing liquor. Mango trees are also found in abundance, the fruits of which are eaten away by the numerous monkeys found in the valley. The Bharias, however, prepare a kind of edible flour out of the mango seeds. The forests also contain clumps of bamboos and many species of other trees. Numerous herbs and medicinal plants, which the Bharias know as cures for certain ailments, remain largely unidentified and unexploited.

The fauna

The Patalkot valley is not very well stocked with game, though there is reason to believe that at one time it was. The Bharias maintain that due to occasional forest fires and also burning of forest patches for *dahiya* cultivation, wild animals have almost disappeared from the vicinity of their villages. Yet, there are tigers in Patalkot, though their number may be small. During the summer and winter seasons these animals keep themselves hidden in the thick forests of Doodhi and Gaini rivers, but before and during the rains they make their appearance occasionally at unexpected places. The Bharias refer to the tiger as *lampuchhiya*, the long-tailed or *janwar* (animal). The tiger is regarded as a deity and *baghdeo* is worshipped annually, or on suitable occasions, to keep the Bharias "free from its deadly teeth and claws". The leopard or *cheeta*, which is often referred to as *chitwa* by the Bharias, as though it were a pet dog, is more dangerous. There are a good many leopards in Patalkot.

Bears are uncommon in the valley; they are said to roam outside, in the forests between Atariya and Bamhni. Deer are seen occasionally but they are not found in large numbers. The animal, rarely seen though, is the wild bear. Numerous are the black-faced monkeys which move about in groups and may be seen almost anywhere in the forest of Patalkot. They are constantly driven away from the fields but seldom killed although they are responsible for causing great damage to the crops. Wild cats are rather many and a menace to fowls.

Among the birds may be mentioned the rock and green pigeons, bulbuls, crows and babblers. There are snakes of various kinds which make their appearance during the summer and rains. The more dangerous, however, are the black and brown scorpions which may creep down the walls of a Bharia house unexpectedly. In the forests, the Bharias are able to locate the bee combs and rob them of their honey and wax.

Fish are fairly abundant in the rivers. While fishing is a regular pastime with the Bharias, hunting has ceased to be important in their life.

Communications

Patalkot can be reached only by road and by undertaking a foot journey down to the valley. One must go to Tamia, a place which is situated 56 km away from Chhindwara, the district headquarters, or, better still, stop at Bijori, a village about 4 km from Tamia. Bijori is an important roadside village. It has a dakbungalow, and a church built in the latter part of the 19th century which was formerly under the control of the Evangelical National Missionary Society of Stockholm. From here a *katcha* (fair-weather) road goes towards Harrai, the headquarters of the erstwhile Harrai Jagir which comprised the Patalkot valley. The road from Bijori to Harrai is about 76 km but in good condition only up to Chhindi—the marketplace frequented by the Bharias—and a village with a number of Muslim households.

From Bijori the road ascends to the Bijori Ghat and then runs until near the 16 km sign where a bifurcation on the left shows the path to Patalkot. In fair weather a jeep can go up to this place, very near Bijadhana village, and even to a further distance of a few furlongs that lead to the top edge of the valley. From there one has to go down to the bottom on foot. The valley was well connected with narrow stone steps, built during the visit of the Rashtrapati, late Dr. Rajendra Prasad. But with the passage of time, from the early 1950s, the stone steps have thoroughly damaged by the rains and landslides so that it has now become difficult to go down or climb up the valley. At places, one is left to negotiate the rocks and may take half an hour to reach the first village in the valley.

Owing to extension of forest activities and movement of heavy trucks in the open season, the *katcha* road from Bijori to Chhindi has been improved. A bus of the State Road Transport Corporation, popularly known as "halting", plies between Chhindwara and Tamia, and may at times run up to Chhindi during "fair weather". The forest contractors have laid tracks for the use of trucks from Batra village up to the forest coupes situated near Jad and Malini villages inside Patalkot. Inside the valley, one has to walk to reach a Bharia village. Foot tracks run through the hills to such villages as Chimtipur and Dudipatha, Kaream, Pachgol, Harrakachar, Jadmandal and Malini. A visitor without a guide, however, is likely to lose his way; one may begin his journey for a Bharia village and end it on the river bank where the Bharias fish.

The Bharias, however, use their traditionat forest tracks while visiting different villages with confidence and without difficulty. They are familiar with almost all important hill features on the different routes. These tracks climb up and down the steep hills and while going down the river valleys one has to support himself with the roots of trees and creepers to avoid falling down the cliff. The tracks leading out of the Patalkot valley are no less difficult. On the west and north-west of the valley, the Bharias use the Bordia ghat, Pipal ghat, Mohua ghat, Pinsa ghat and Khuta ghat tracks; on the west they make use of Chimtipur ghat and Dongra ghat; on the northern side they traverse Karrapani and Amdhana ghat.

Historical perspective

Very little is known of the Satpura plateau and its people, particularly the Bharias, in the annals of the history relating to the early centuries. The archaeological findings of copper plates at Seoni and Chhindwara combined with others in the Ajanta caves indicate that a line of Rajput princes of the Vakataka dynasty was ruling the Satpura plateau from the third century. The founder of this dynasty, in all probability, was Vindhya Sakti whose capital was at Bandak in Chanda (the present Chandrapur). According to Dr Buhler this dynasty might have lasted from the end of the third to the middle of the sixth century and, according to Dr Fleet's[7] hypothesis, from the fifth to the eighth century. However, the famous Chinese pilgrim Huen Tsiang, who visited Chanda district in A.D. 639 makes no mention of this dynasty, and, therefore, it seems improbable that the Vakataka kingdom could have been in existence at that time.

The Satpura plateau including the Patalkot valley might have formed part of the Gaur kingdom (Gaur being the classical term for Uttar Pradesh and Bengal). General Cunningham[8] derives the name of the Gonds from the Gaur kingdom that came to be known to the Muhammedans as the Gondwana. Practically nothing is known of the various rulers and the rules of this area until the emergence of the Gond kingdom at Deogarh sometime in the last decade of the 16th century. The capital of the Gond dynasty at Deogarh was a fortress, the ruins of which exist about 24 miles south-west of Chhindwara where it is situated on a crest of the hills. According to the popular tradition the Gaoli kings preceded the kingdom of Gonds. The tradition lays it that the semi-mythical Gond hero Jataba, founder of the Gond dynasty, who was born from a virgin under a bean plant, and was magically protected by a cobra while its mother was away, took service under the twin Gaoli kings. The story goes that he gained the favour of Gaoli kings by the feat of lifting the large castle gate off its hinges with his bare hands. He was ordered to kill a buffalo at the next Diwali festival, but did not know how to do it. The Goddess, *Devi*, however, appeared to him in a dream and told him that when the proper moment came his wooden stick would change into a sword, and that after killing the buffalo he should kill the Gaoli kings seated on the royal elephant and thus establish himself as the ruler. Jataba was able to do so and thus became the popular hero of the Gond tribe. His name is still held in high esteem in the tribal legends. Jataba's name is mentioned in the *Ain-i-Akbari* which confirms that he was a ruler of the area at that time.

The third or fourth in the dynasty was a prince called Bakhat Buland who was reigning in A.D. 1700. He is said to have gone to Delhi and entered the service of Aurangzeb. It is said that he made the emperor happy with his feats who in turn induced him to abandon the rites of Bhim Sen and to adopt the Muhammedan faith. Thereafter, he was acknowledged as the Raja of Deogarh. During his reign he set about to develop his kingdom. According to Sir Richard Jenkins,[9] "He employed indiscriminately Musalmans and Hindus of ability to introduce order and regularity into his immediate domain. Industrious settlers from all quarters were attracted to Gondwana, many thousands of villages were founded, and agriculture, manufacture and even commerce made considerable advances. It may be said that much of the success of the Maratha administration was owing to the groundwork established by him." Bakhat Buland added considerable territory to his dominion including Seoni, Katangi, Chhapra and Dongartal. He was the founder of the modern city of Nagpur. At this time the kingdom of Chanda and Deogarh were attached to the *Subah* of Berar. Towards the end of Aurangzeb's reign, when the empire had grown weak due to long-drawn wars against the Marathas, Bakhat Buland was known to have plundered the Mughul territory.

The next Raja of Deogarh was Chand Sultan who made his capital at Nagpur. Under him the country prospered. He died in 1739 and there were quarrels leading to usurpation of the throne by an illegitimate son of Bakhat Buland. Chand Sultan's widow requested help from Raghuji Bhonsla of Berar in the interest of her sons. Dissensions, however, continued between the brothers and in 1843 Burhan Shah, son of Chand Sultan, was practically made a state pensionary, whereas the real power passed to the Maratha chief. After this event the history of Deogarh kingdom is not chronicled.

Up to 1803 the Maratha administration was, on the whole, satisfactory and the country prospered under their rule. During that year Raghuji II joined the Sindhia against the East India Company but both were defeated by the British at Assaye and Argaon. By the treaty of Deogaon, the Marathas had to cede almost one-third of their territory to the British. To make up the losses the Marathas imposed new taxes at the time. It was during this period that the poor Bharias living in Bhardagarh and other parts of the *Jagir* area receded to the then inaccessible valley of Patalkot. The Gond hill-chiefs finding a favourable opportunity came down from their mountain fortresses and plundered the country. In 1818 the British defeated the Bhonsla prince Appa Saheb in the battle of Sitabaldi. They deposed him but, while he was being taken to Allahabad, he managed to escape and hid in Mahadeo hills. In Patalkot, a huge protruding rock under which 10 to 15 persons can take shelter, known as Raja Khoh, is said to have provided shelter to Appa Saheb after his escape. Later on, Appa Saheb with the help of the Gond Chiefs made an abortive attempt to capture Deogarh, but he lost and escaped to Punjab. The name of the valley, Patalkot, seems to have originated from this incident. ('*Patal*' meaning nether world, and '*kot*' in Marathi 'fort' or a place to hide in or shelter.)

During the minority of Raja Raghuji III, the Nagpur territories were administered from 1818 to 1830 by Sir Richard Jenkins. Captain Montgomery was made the Superintendent of Chhindwara. He established peace and order in the area. The following summary in which he gave the results of his management is worth quoting.[10]

"In conclusion I have only to add that those hilly and mountainous tracts held by the Gond tributaries, where murders and thefts were neither accounted criminal nor sinful; through which before our management no individual of respectability could pass in safely, if at all, from which hordes of banditti used to be poured down on the fertile valley of the Nerbudda and the *haveli* lands of Betul and Seoni to plunder and distress their more peaceful inhabitants, to drive off their heirs and rock and burn their villages; these are now the abode of comparative contentment and industry, and I may with truth, confidence and satisfaction assure you that a great change has been effected. Population has been partially restored and is gradually increasing; no traveller or stranger has fallen a victim for six years to the cupidity of the lawless freebooters; no complaint has been made against the inhabitants by my neighbours of the Honourable Company's territory who are on three sides of me; cultivation is improving and comfort is evident among them; and they profess openly their preference for the life they now lead to that from which I had little hope of ever winning them."

In 1853 after the death of Raghuji III, the Maratha territories were taken over by the British. In 1858, the Zamindar of Harrokot joined the forces of the famous revolutionary Tantia Tope, but lost and consequently his *jagir* was confiscated.

While a great part of the Satpura Plateau including the Patalkot valley was under the Gond kings and later on under the Marathas, there were, in fact, several Gond chieftains who weilded authority over the area under a feudal system. According to Sir R. Jenkins[11] "the unproductiveness of the hills and the forests and natural strength of the country preserved these chiefs from entire subjugation to the Marathas who, however, possessed themselves of the most accessible parts and whose policy generally was to support one of the most powerful of them to keep the others in check, and to be responsible for the depredations they were always in the habit of committing on the neighbouring plains".

Almod and Bharadagarh *jagirs* had originated in a grant given by the Gond Raja Jatba Sha as a reward for suppressing certain hill chiefs. A record held by the Harrai family describes the gradual acquisition at various times of the land which formed the Harrai, Sonpur and Pratabgarh-Pagara *jagirs*. As a rule the Gond Rajas did not require money payment but the chieftains or *jagirdars* were supposed to punish the marauders, be loyal to the Raja and enjoy a service tenure. The Marathas, it appears, made unreasonable demands at times and the tribals such as the Bharias were required to go to more and more inaccessible hills as they were unable to pay the *Takoli* (*nazrana*).

When the British took over the administration they recognised the important *jagirs*. *Sanads* were granted to the *jagirdars* of Harrai (Patalkot valley was part of the Harrai *jagir*), Pagara and to certain other *jagirdars*. From 1867 to 1874 certain changes were made. The *sanads* were reissued with new conditions. The *jagirdar* were allowed income from rents, lease, excises, pounds, unclaimed property, sale of timber and minor forest produce; and were allowed and required to maintain their own police. These *sanads*, however, were not issued until 1897. Further changes were made and in 1902 excise and police jurisdiction of *jagirdars* were resumed by the government. After Independence the *jagirdars* have completely lost their power of collecting revenue.

The people

Origin of the Bharias: Patalkot has a total population of 700; of which 604 belong to the Bharia tribe and the rest (96) are Gonds.

The Bharias of Patalkot call themselves "Bharia", as distinguished from those Bharias who live away from Patalkot and its neighbourhood, and who prefer to call themselves "Bharia-Bhumiya". The word Bhumiya means "owner, lord, or master" of the soil but the meaning of the word Bharia is obscure. If it is taken that the word is formed *bhar* meaning weight or load it would simply mean that the Bharias were so called because they were load-carriers, or coolies. While no tribe would like to be referred to by a derogatory term, in all probability this term was coined for the people by others who considered themselves superior.

In any case, the Bharias have long since forgotten their original affinities. One of the stories of origin runs to the effect that "Arjun, when matters were going badly with the Pandavas in their battle against the Kauravas, took up a handful of *bharru* grass and, pressing it, produced a host of men who fought in the battle and became the ancestors or the Bharias."[12]

Russel and Hiralal consider that "there is no reason to doubt that Bharia is the contemptuous form of Bhar . . . and that the Bharias belong to the great Bhar tribe who were once dominant in the eastern part of the United Provinces, but are now at the bottom of the social scale, and relegated by their conquerors to the degrading office of swineherds."[13] While this may be broadly true, of the affinities of the Bharias, the Patalkot Bharias certainly do not rear swine. They, however, definitely consider themselves to have been related to the Gonds in the past. A myth recorded in Rated, and known to the Bharias of Patalkot villages, supports this contention.

"The Gonds (called *Koi* or *Bhoi*) and Bharias were brothers. They were born of two mothers but of the same father. The mother of the Bharias was in the habit of stealing food and was, therefore, called *Bhadiyayi* or *Bhariyayi* (*Ayi* in the Marathi language means mother). One day they all decided to go to 'Deo-Khiriyan' or place of worship. The senior wife went ahead with her children but the junior wife and children were left behind. The former, while climbing the place of worship, said, let her be left behind. She is a *Bhariyayi*. Thus she was left behind and her children were called Bhariya, the Children of *Bhadiyayi* or *Bhariyayi*.

Physical appearance

In physical appearance an average Bharia appears somewhat dark complexioned with medium stature and well-built body capable of living the difficult life of the hills. The physical characteristics are reported to have been studied scientifically by certain anthropologists but their results have not been published and no description, therefore, of their (Bharia) anthropometry is available. A keen observer can, however, recognise two distinct physical types among the Bharias. One is characterised by dark complexion, tall, muscular build with large limbs. Such persons usually have large bright eyes. The root of their nose is somewhat flat and the nostrils extended. The other type is marked by wheatish complexion, somewhat slim physique, shorter stature, and eyes dullwhite lying in deep sockets. The women who come from such villages as Sidholi and Batka-Khapa area are usually dark in complexion and resemble the Gonds of the neighbourhood rather than the Bharias of the Patalkot valley. It is certain that there has been considerable miscegenation of Gond blood among the Bharias so that the tribe has now lost its original racial characteristics.

The Bharias, on the whole, cannot be said to be good-looking people even though there are exceptions. The rigour of the natural habitat and its climate are a great drain on the strength of the Bharias who lack proper nourishment. Effects of liquor and absence of medical facilities often sap the vitality of the young quickly and the Bharias, therefore, often appear more in agethan they really are. Both men and women, however, are capable of undertaking hard work than their counter-parts in the plains.

Demography

Villages: The confines of the Patalkot valley have 13 inhabited villages covering an area of 4,457.10 acres. The villages are scattered and located at a distance of four to seven kilometres from one another. Almost 75 per cent of the valley is covered with forests.

In the 13 villages of the valley are distributed 91 households belonging to the Bharia tribe and 21 belonging to the Gond tribe.

Population: In proportion to the 31-sq. mile area of Patalkot, the total population of Patalkot is only 700 according to the latest figures collected (at the time of this study) for the 1971 Census. Density of population works out to about 10 per sq km (It is 178 per sq km for the country and 94 per sq km for the state.) The total population of the valley is shown in Table 1.

TABLE 1: **Total population of the Patalkot valley**

Name of village/ Village group	No. of households	Population		
		Males	Females	Total
Khamarpur, Sehara, Pachgol	25	79	74	153
Jadmandal, Harrakachhar	26	88	77	165
Ziran, Dodipara	1	1	1	2
Chimtipur	15	28	36	64
Sukhabund, Harmau	8	24	29	53
Ghogri, Gujadongri	1	2	2	4
Kaream, Rated	36	138	121	259
Total	112	360	340	700

This population also includes 96 Gonds who live in 21 households and form less then one-seventh of the total population of the valley.

Population variation: Population in the Patalkot valley over a period of three decades increased from 567 in 1941 to 700 in 1971. The Census figures for the years 1941 to 1971 persented in Table 2 show the population variation.

TABLE 2: **Population variation in three decades, 1941-1971**

Year	Population	Variation
1941	567	
1951	600	+33
1961	675	+75
1971	700	+25

There have been fluctuations in the rise in population between 1941 and 1971 as is evident from the above Table. During the period of 30 years the increase in population is only 133. The lowest increase in population is from 1961-71. It is difficult to attribute any definite reason for the slow growth of increase, as no proper data are available in this regard. This could, however, be due to reasons such as high mortality (owing to lack of medical facilities), low fertility, emigration in search of work, etc.

Bharias and Gonds

In the neighbourhood of the Patalkot valley the most predominant tribal group is the Gond. As has been mentioned earlier, the Gond kingdom of Deogarh came into existence in the 16th century. During this time, the Bharias and the Gonds settled in the hills due to the large influx of Hindu settlers in the plains below the Satpura Plateau. The Gonds and Bharias thus appear to have been living in close contact with each other for about, four centuries, if not more. The Gonds, however, belonged to the ruling class. Being numerically strong and more aggressive than the Bharias, the Gond culture seems to have greatly influenced the life and thought of the Bharias. On the other hand, the dominant culture of the Hindus influenced the culture of the Gonds and Bharias alike. This could be a reason as to why the Gonds and the Bharias have common culture traits, whether these be their original traits or imbibed from the Hindus. A reference to such similarities, as are predominant in the two tribal societies, is relevant here.

Material culture of the Gonds and the Bharias presents great similarity. The dress, utensils, implements and tools used by them are similar. The Gonds are, however, comparatively well off than the Bharias as is evident from their clothes and utensils. A turban is an essential item of dress among the Gonds and Bharias. The Gond and Bharia houses are, by and large, of the same type though the rich Gonds have larger and better houses than those of the Bharias. Both smoke *chilams* and carry with them flint and a piece of steel to ignite fire. The food and its preparation and the method of cooking are the same, though here again, one would naturally find the Gonds slightly better off. The *pej* or gruel, which is part of the daily food, has the same significance for a Bharia as for a Gond. The importance of liquor in the two tribal societies is alike: both the tribes indulge in drinking and often distill their own liquor despite stringent excise rules and the fear of officials.

The Gonds and the Bharias are organised into totemic clans called *gots*. Some of the *gots* being *bhaiband* and others *mamu bhanja*.[14] Clan exogamy is practised. Both the societies have their tribal panchayats in which older members of the community participate and decide the disputes of civil nature. The tribal panchayat still remains an important institution in both the tribes.

The Bharia rules of marriage, more or less, follow the Gond pattern. Both practise *lamjhana*. Cross-cousin marriage is an important feature of both. Among the Gonds cross-cousin marriage is obligatory so that a person who has given his daughter to another person usually insists that the latter give a girl in marriage to his son. This custom is known an *doodth lautana* or return of milk.[15] The Bharias also follow the custom but do not carry it to that extent. Among the Gonds if the sister's daughter marries a person other than the son of her maternal uncle, the latter may even claim "milk money", which may be nominal, say, Rs. 5. This is a sort of compensation which may be paid to him because he loses the girl who could have been his son's wife.

There is also great similarity between the two tribes in the realm of religion. "The Gods are much the same as those of the Gonds and are represented by iron in some shape." *Baradeo*, the great god of the Gonds, is the same as the *Baradeo* of the Bharias. Any vow taken in the name of *Baradeo* is as sacred to the Gond as to the Bharia. The *saj* tree (Terminalla tomentosa) is held sacred by both the Gonds and the Bharias, with the only difference that the Patalkot Bharias go to the tree to perform a rite, whereas the Gonds would usually bring a branch of the tree and plant it near the house for the purpose of worship. Such deities as *Matiya* and *Baghdeo*, which are really the products of tribal religion, are worshipped by both. The *bidri* rite, which is performed to secure the blessings of the deities for the purpose of reaping a good harvest, is an important rite for both the Gonds and the Bharias. The Gonds of Bijadhana and Thanakhera whose agricultural land is adjacent to Patalkot perform this rite annually with the Bharias of Rated.

A comparative study of the two cultures would bring out many more similarities between them. Here, however, the main object is to show that the two cultures are not essentially dissimilar to each other. Indeed, the Gond and Hindu traits are so predominant among the Bharias that it is difficult to say what Bharia culture was originally like.

A discussion of the dissimilar traits, however, would also be necessary at this stage. The first of these is the dialect. The Gondi dialect as spoken by the Gonds of Betul and Chhindwara has made no great impact on the Bharias. Though many of them are able to understand it, they certainly do not use it as their tongue.[16] Within the family group and with the relatives Bharias use a dialect which certainly bears no resemblance to Gondi.

According to Russel, the Bharias speak Hindi, and profess not to know a word of Gondi, though always living as neighbours with Gonds.[17] Among the Gonds there are many clans grouped according to the number of gods, often five or seven which a family worships. A man from a family worshipping five gods may marry a girl only in a family worshipping seven gods, and vice versa. In respect of exogamy, in the opinion of Russel, "The Gonds appear to preserve traces of the system found in Australia, by which the whole tribe is split into two or four main divisions, and every man in one or two of them must marry a woman in the other one or two."[18] But while the Bharias equate some of their clans with those of the Gonds, and even though members of two clans may have fraternal or *bhai band* relations, there is no system of clan grouping according to the number of gods among the Bharias. In fact, for most of them, clan is the only unit of exogamy.

Finally, there is the difference of status and commensality between the two tribes. The Gonds consider themselves superior to Bharias, economically and socially, and it is of some importance that the Bharias accept this position. In tribal societies usually an ethnocentric tribe may claim superiority to another but the latter in turn may consider the former as inferior. In the inter-community relations between the Gonds and Bharias, however, the superior position claimed by the Gonds is not challenged. Bharias do not intermarry with Gonds, but if either take a wife from the other, the offence is atoned for by giving a dinner, and the offspring is legitimate, and belongs to the caste of the father.[19] The Gonds do not eat with the Bharias. The Bharias, however, accept food and water from the Gonds without hesitation.

REFERENCES AND NOTES

1,2,3. Russell, R.V. (ed.), *Central Provinces District Gazetteers, Chhindwara District*, Bombay, 1907, p. 2.
4. Russell, R.V., op. cit. pp. 7-8.
5. Russell R.V., op. cit. pp. 7-8
6,7. Russell, R.V., op. cit. p. 24.
8. Ibid., p. 24.
9. Russel, R.V., op. cit. p. 29.
10. Russell, R.V. op. cit. pp. 32-33.
11. Russell, R.V., op. cit.
12. Russell and Hiralal, *The Tribes and Castes of the Central Provinces of India*. Vol. II (London, 1916), p. 242. Today no such myth is known to the Bharias of Patalkot. They worship the Pandavas, however.
13. Ibid., p. 243.
14. Ruesell, R.V., op. cit. p. 70.
15. Kurup, A.M., *Glimpses of the Life and Culture of the Tribes of Madhya Pradesh*, Vanyajati Vol. V., 1962.
16. Russell, R.V., op. cit. pp. 70-71.
17. Russell, R.V., op. cit. p. 70.
18. Russell and Hiralal, Vol. II, op. cit. p. 64.
19. Ibid., p. 70.

2

MATERIAL CULTURE

FOR THE past 20 years or so, the Bharias of Patalkot have been leading a more settled life. This has helped to enrich their material culture. From time immemorial they have been in contact, though limited, with the Gonds and other Hindu communities residing in the surrounding villages of the valley. They have had, and still have, contacts with the traders and merchants in their villages and also at Chhindi, where a weekly market is held for the past 50 years. Often they come in contact with the officials of the Forest, Revenue and Police Departments. Physical communications have always played an important part in culture change. The *katcha* road opened recently for forest exploitation has made a tremendous impact on the Bharias of Patalkot. They are now in close contact with the labourers from the plains and forest contractors engaged in cutting and removing timber. The increased communication facilities and incoming of outsiders have made a marked impact on the Bharia material culture.

House and its design

Before starting construction of a house an auspicious site is selected by the *Bhumka* (the priest). This site is sanctified by offering oblations and prayers.

The construction begins with the placing of *barendi*; a central horizontal pole measuring 16 to 18 feet, on the *thambo*, that is, two supporting poles fixed at a distance of about 14 feet. The height of these is about 10 feet, from the ground. On both sides of the *barendi*, at a distance of about 8 feet, parallel poles called *thareli*, of same length as *barendi*, are placed on the two supporting poles called *thumiya* which are 6 feet high from the ground. *Thareli* poles are shorter than *thambo* poles so that there is a regular slope in the roof on both sides to allow free flow of rain-water. *Malgas* or vertical beams are placed in such a way that one end is tied to *barendi* and the other to *thareli*. On these *malgas* (bamboos) are spread all over the roof and tied with tree bark. After completion of the frame the roof is thatched either with *bharai* (grass) or country tiles. The thatched roof is invariably thick, as much as 12 inches to prevent leakage during the rains. Walls are constructed with split bamboo to enclose the living room called *bhatar* the length of which is about 14 feet and width not more than 8 feet. The walls are plastered on both sides with a mixture of clay, cowdung and water. A second coat of *chhui matti* (white clay) is applied to these walls. The wooden door-frames are fixed in the centre of the front wall as well as the back walls of the living room. If there is no provision for a *usari* (verandah) behind the living room, one door-frame in the front serves the purpose of entrance and exit.

The Bharias also construct a bamboo ceiling called *mandha* below the roof for keeping heavy baskets and other articles of use. A *mandha* ceiling keeps the room cool during summer. For reaching the *mandha* they use *naseni*, a temporary ladder made of bamboo.

The roof

Formerly the Bharias thatched their roofs invariably with grass. But now many families construct houses with tiled (*khapra*) roofs. Out of 112 houses in the valley, 51 have tiled roofs. In 17 houses of Rated village only three to four houses are having thatched roofs. It is said that during early 1960s, one Shankar of Lotia village married a girl named Dukribai, daughter of Budhi Bharia of Rated. After marriage he lived with his father-in-law at Rated, and learnt the technique of making tiles.

Shankar now charges Rs. 50 to Rs. 100 (depending upon the quality) for preparing tiles for a house. Some prosperous families use tiles even on *gothas* or cattle-sheds. Use of tiles has almost become a status symbol with the Bharias. Chamru Bharia of Kaream used tiles on the *gotha* attached to his house. He paid Rs. 50 to Jhendu Gond of Thanakheda for making tiles for him. Guddan of Harrakachhar had prepared tiles for Rs. 150 for Trilok Bharia. Now many young Bharia men like Bala, Forelal and Janmusingh have also learnt the art of preparing tiles. Halku Patel of Rated is now thinking of using "English tiles" (factory-made tiles) for his house. He said that tiled roofs were better because periodical change of grass-thatch could be avoided. The Bharias say that the estimated cost of a tile-roofed house varied from Rs. 900 to Rs. 1,200. Nevertheless many people still believe that grass-thatched roof are cheaper and better than tiled roofs. They feel that leakage of rainwater from the grass-thatched roof can easily be repaired by placing a little grass, whereas it takes longer to replace the tiles. This is one example where the work of a single artisan has affected the natural culture of the people.

A roof with a slope on two sides only is the common pattern in Patalkot today, that is 1976 when the last visit was made. A few houses constructed recently have roofs with four-sided slopes. Premlal constructed his new house four years ago with a roof having slopes on four sides. This is a new design in tribal architecture borrowed by the Bharias. The roof with a two-side slope is being replaced by a four-side slope. All this change in house construction could be attributed to their frequent visits to the huts of the Gonds outside the Valley.

Doors and windows

Fifty years or so ago the Bharia houses had no doors. They closed the entrance with a sliding piece of *tatta* (bamboo mat). But now a days most of the Bharia houses have wooden doors. These doors do not have sufficient height with the result that an entrant is required to stoop low before he can enter the living room. Although the Bharias have started using door-frames in place of the bamboo mat, the size of the entrance has not much changed. The lowest level of the roof is also not more than five feet from the ground. Nowadays one can also see the wooden doors with certain rectangular designs carved on them. Arrangement for securing the doors with a hook and chain called *kadi-konda* is also common. When the Bharias go out they lock their doors. This arrangement ensures security of their household possessions which are increasing day-by-day. In spite of houses having windows they are not kept open for ventilation. There is no provision even for the smoke to escape except through the thatch.

Size of house

The Bharia houses were very small in size. But now the average size of a Bharia house is 14′×14′×9′. The walls are made of woven bamboo splits and plastered on both sides with a mixture of clay and cow-dung. Occasionally they smear the mud walls with *chhui matti* and the walls are at times decorated with beautiful designs, using *geru* (a kind of brick coloured clay). Some houses in Rated also have designs on the front wall of their houses.

A Bharia house consists of one living room called *bhitar* and one open front verandah called *usari*. A few houses have been designed to have *usari* on the front and back sides of the living room. In the front, there is a small courtyard called *angan*. The floor of the house remains *katcha* and is given a coat of cow-dung and water mixture every week to keep its surface plain and smooth. Now a days *usari* (verandah) is enclosed by raised walls and the entrance is located at the centre. Thus *usari* also serves as a drawing room. The average size of the door-frame is about 4′×1½′. The living room is used as kitchen during the day and as a bedroom during the night. Two-storeyed houses in Patalkot are non-existent. Halku Patel had constructed a small two-storeyed house a few years back, but due to the fury of wind and heavy rains it could not survive long and ultimately collapsed.

The interior and exterior parts of the Bharia house present

a neat and tidy appearance. They are swept twice or thrice during the day by a *khareta* (a kind of grass broom). The Bharias throw the refuse in the adjacent *bari* (kitchen garden) and the rubbish heap is used as manure.

When the house warming ceremony is held the Bharia gives a feast to his neighbours and close relatives who have helped in the construction of the house.

There is a general belief that a house must not face the east, as it may bring prolonged illness and disease in the family. However, now there is some change in the facing of a house. Hori, son of Lodha Bharia, has constructed his house facing east but the entrance in the *angan* is from the north. Tedhu, son of Dhori Bharia, was constructing his house during my visit and his new house also faced east. On inquiry, he said he had seen many houses facing east outside his settlement and people living in such houses were happy and healthy. Such changes in the attitudes of the Bharias and consequently in the structure of their houses is due to their contact with the outside world.

The courtyard

In front of the Bharia houses, one comes across a clean and neat courtyard known as *angan*. In this the Bharias erect *mandha* and *tonga*. The top platform of the *mandha* is generally used for keeping grass or for drying *mahua* grains, etc., in the sun; grains being stored in baskets made of *mahua* leaves called *pudi*.

Tonga is errected for keeping maize corns to be used for the next sowing season. It is raised by fixing one pole in the centre and four poles around it. The upper ends of these four poles meet above the central pole. These poles are given support by buckling one end of the bamboo to these poles and the other end to a central pole.

Cattle shed

Every house has a *goatha*, an enclosure for keeping cattle, attached to the dwelling unit. The structure of a *goatha* is the same as that of a house without *usari*. Instead of plastered walls a *goatha* is enclosed on all sides with bamboo sticks and a small entrance is kept at one end. Generally the roof of the *goatha* is thatched with grass but recently some families have used tiles. Chintaman Bharia and Bondal Bharia have used tiles for covering the roof of *goathas* attached to their houses. Chamru of Kaream has also covered his *goatha* with tiles though the roof of his dwelling house is thatched with grass.

The size and shape of the *manda* and *tonga* differ from house to house but the purpose for which they are constructed is the same. These have not undergone any structural change for the past two generations. *Manda* and *tonga* have persisted since time immemorial. It appears that earlier these were used for storing forest produce but now for storing agricultural produce.

Household articles

The simple design and small size of the houses of the Bharias in former generations, and also their frequent change from one *Dahiya* field to another, suggest fewer and invaluable possessions of household articles. Now the Bharias are leading a settled life and have regular contact with outsiders. A Bharia of ordinary means tries to acquire as many articles of household use as possible within his meagre earnings. The following are some of the important material possessions:

Grain containers: The Bharias use one or two big grain containers about five feet high. The containers are placed in the living room in such a manner that it gets divided into two small portions. The container is called *bakhara* or *dulha*. It is woven out of a bamboo frame and plastered with mud. The other type, called *kothi* is made of pure mud mixed with husk. The average size of container is about 5 feet high and 2½ feet in diameter. It is usually kept on a *madachi*, a wooden stool, or an earthen platform. The two portions are used as bedroom and storeroom. It also facilitates comfortable stay of guests.

Mortar and Pestle: In every house there is a wooden *okhali* (mortar) fixed in one of the suitable corners of a room. The

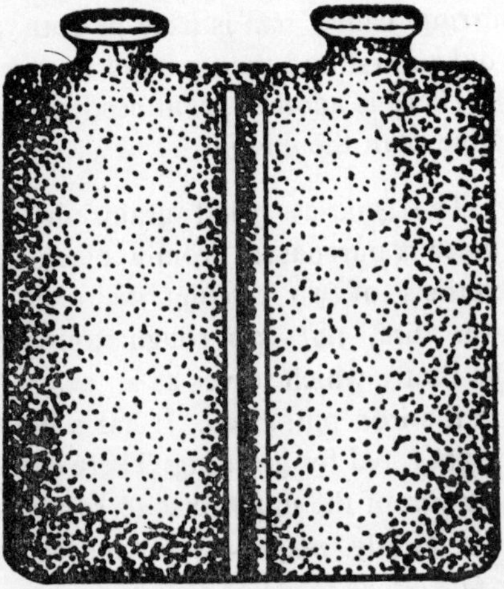

Kothi

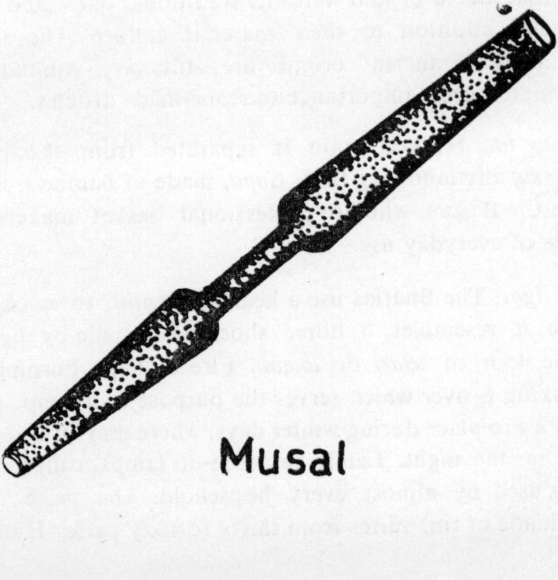

Musal

Bharia women use *musal* (pestle) to pound grain. A *musal* is a thick and long cylindrical wooden stick with a depression around its middle for providing proper grip while husking grain. An iron-ring called *sam* is fixed at both ends. Grain is husked in the *okhali* first and then ground in a *chakia* or *kuleta* (stone grinder). There is another grain pestle called *girni* which is smaller in shape than the *musal*

Grinding stone: The Bharias grind grains in a stone-grinder, *chakia*. The grinder is purchased from a black-smith for Rs. 8 to Rs. 10. It consists of two circular discs kept one upon the other. The lower disc, *tali* is of rough stone with an iron pin *khuti* fixed at the centre which serves as an axle. The upper disc, *mur*, rotates on the iron pin, *khuti*. It has a hole in the centre through which grain is fed for grinding. There is a wooden handle fixed on the outer rim of the upper disc to rotate it. In addition to the *chakia* a family may possess another grinding-stone called *kuleta* or *jata*. It is made of clay and is used for grinding soft grains like *kodo* or *kutki*. The design of *kuleta* is the same as that of the *chakia* with the difference that the central pin of *kuleta* is made of bamboo. The Bharias possess a stone slab called *seel* and a stone roller called *lodha* or grinding spices. It appears that *kuleta* or *jata* were the traditional ones and *chakia* was a later addition to their material culture. The *seel* and *lodha*, though of ancient origin, are still very common. The Bharias attach great importance to stone-made articles.

Winnowing fan: Husked grain is separated from the bran by using a *supa* (winnowing fan). *Supa*, made of bamboo, is bought from the Basors, who are professional basket makers. It is an article of everyday use.

Fire and light: The Bharias use a hearth, *angathi*, to cook food. In shape it resembles a horse shoe and is made by digging a pit on the floor of *usari* or *angan*. Fire is kept burning even after cooking is over which serves the purpose of a lamp. It also serves as a fire-place during winter days, where they sit and gossip till late in the night. Lately kerosene-oil lamps, called *chimni*, are being used by almost every household. The price of the *chimni* (made of tin) varies from thirty to sixty paise. Hurricane

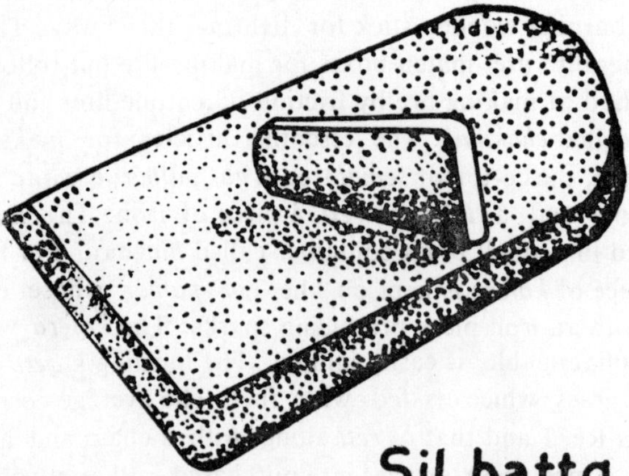

Sil batta

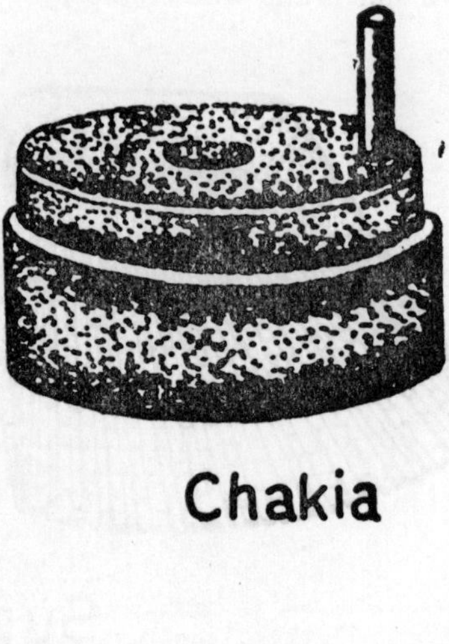

Chakia

lanterns, however, are not found in the houses of the Bharias living in the Valley, because they cannot afford kerosene oil. The Bharias, while going from one place to another in the night, carry a burning wooden stick for lighting their way. They do not generally use match-boxes for making fire but follow their old method of making fire by friction of a stone-flint and a piece of iron called *chakmak*. The essential articles for making fire are: *kafera*, the cotton of *semal* tree, a *gar pathar*, a white shining stone-flint, and a *loha* or *reti*, a piece of iron. The *kafera* is preserved in a small brass container called *hingawa*. For making fire a piece of *kafera* is kept on the *gar pathar* whose edge is struck with an iron piece producing sparks. The *kafera* which is highly inflammable is easily ignited. The burning *kafera* is kept on dry grass which is fed with fuel. The average cost of the *hingwa* is Re. 1 and that of *reti* along with a chain and hook is Rs. 1.50. Once these articles are purchased a Bharia would not incur any expenditure for making fire. This is more economical than the match-box. Thus the old practice of making fire by lint-and steel still persists in Patalkot. The practice of keeping fire round the clock is still in vogue though they keep *chakmak* and are aware of the use of match-box. This, according to them, is to ward off evil spirits and wild animals.

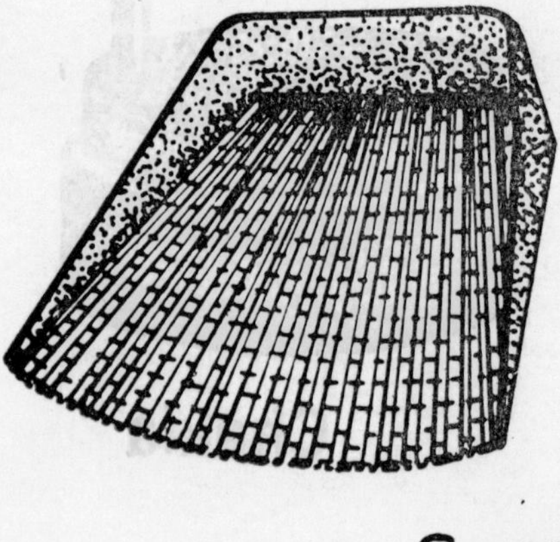

Supa

Furniture: The Bharias do not possess any cots, chairs or tables. Some Bharias know how to make bamboo-cots but only a few attempt to make these since it is alleged that these are taken away by Government officials without any payment.

Chakmak

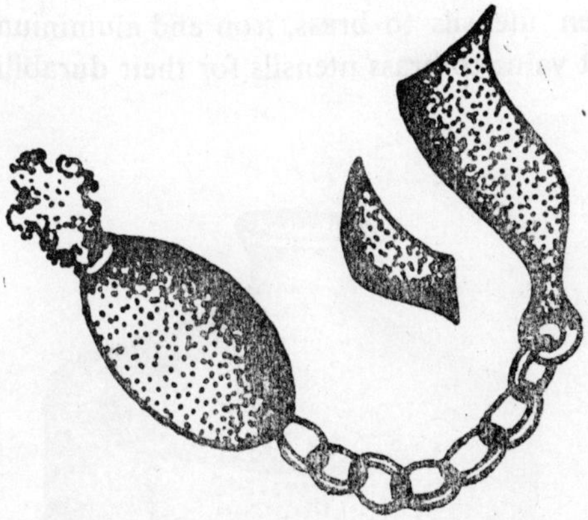

Bedding: The Bharias do not use cots for sleeping as stated above. They sleep on the floor and cover their body and face with a *dhoti* or *sari*. During winter they use rough blankets. Persons having more than two sets of *dhoti* or *sari* use one set as bedspread on the floor. Some poor Bharias use one half portion of a *dhoti* or *sari* for sleeping on and the other half for covering themselves.

Utensils: The utensils used by the Bharias include new and old varieties. On the one hand they use the primitive types of wooden utensils, bamboo articles and earthern pots and on the other they use brass utensils. They have utensils for eating, drinking and measuring commodities. The Bharias use wooden utensils for taking meals and earthen pots for cooking. For storing water large utensils known as *ghagra* and *kaseri* are used and for taking out water a *charu*, jug made of brass, is used Now they also eat in *thali*—a plate made of brass. Previously, the Bharias cooked food in earthen pots but now at times they use brass and aluminium vessels. In Chintaman's house there are plates made of *kasa* metal. The wooden utensils are *kathot* and *chatwa.* The articles made of bamboo are *takji* (basket) and *supa* (winnowing fan). The *kudav* made of wood is used for measuring grain and *pai* made of iron for measuring small quantities of grains. The baskets made of bamboo are named as *pudi.* The Bharias are now in the process of changing over from earthen and wooden utensils to brass, iron and aluminium ones. They attach great value to brass utensils for their durability.

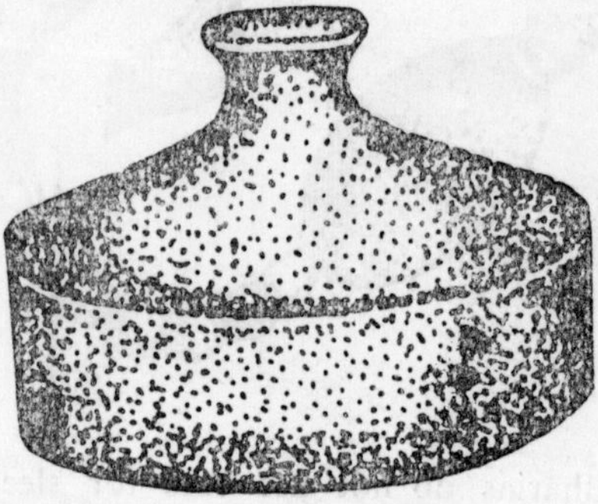

Ghagra

Musical instruments: The musical instruments used by the Bharias are: *dhol*: (drum shaped) made from the wood of *Bijo* tree; *timki*: prepared out of an earthen pot; *basari*: (flute) prepared from bamboo stick and *shikaro*: a single string instrument. *Dhol* and *basari* are most important for synchronising rythm during a dance. Except *shikaro* which is a new addition others have been used since ancient times. *Dhol* is purchased from traders while other musical instruments are made by themselves. It has been observed that the Bharias do not spend money on musical instruments as most of them are home-made. It is only now that *dhol* (drum) is purchased from the market.

Agricultural implements: The Bharias practised only axe-cultivation (shifting cultivation) in the past. An axe called *kulhadi* and a sickle called *hansiya* were the essential implements for such cultivation. Since the Bharias have taken to plough cultivation, *hal* (plough) and *bakhar* are seen in every house A *khanta* (digging stick) is also an essential implement. Some families have now started using iron-spikes instead of *khanta*. The Bharias purchase these implements from blacksmiths and attach them to the wooden pieces made by them. Shift from wooden implements to iron ones has brought a blacksmith among the Bharias. A quick and wide change-over to wooden implements may attract a carpenter to the village and the Bharias, instead of preparing them at home, may depend on him for a few selected fine items in days to come.

Fishing and hunting implements: Though the Bharias are fond of fish, they seldom use any trap or net for catching fish. Even in the present time they continue to use the crude method of catching fish, by mixing poison in water. For this purpose a piece of the bark of *sarai* or *gural* tree is pound and put in the river water. The fish are stupefied and float on the surface of the water in an unconscious state, and are picked up easily. Fishing is done single-handed but occasionally in a family group. Bharias are no more fond of hunting; first, because of the lack of game in the area and, secondly, hunting has been prohibited by the Government. Occasionally however, if a Bharia encounters an animal, he kills it with an axe. An axe is always carried by a Bharia when he goes out to a jungle, alone or in a group. No. special hunting implements are seen with them.

Dress and ornaments

Male dress: The scantiness of Bharia dress is proverbial and the saying goes as *Bharia Bhwaka pwanda langwata* or "the Bharia is verily a devil who only covers his loins with a strip of cloth". This observation of Russell and Hiralal does not hold good now since they lately use more clothing.

The dress of a Bharia consists of a piece of cloth five to seven yards long and about one yard in width called *dhoti* with which he covers his body from waist down to the knees. He covers his chest and the back with *bandi*, half shirt, purchased from the local market. He wraps around the head a sort of turban called *pagri* leaving bare the middle of the head. It is generally three yards in length and half a yard in width. As a rule they never go out barehead. A Bharia man without *pagri* is taken as a widower. He can go without a shirt or *bandi* but not without a *pagri*. At the time of going to bed they take off their *pagri*. A Bharia can be recognised by his *pagri*. Inside the *pagri*. he tucks in his *chilam* (baked earthen tobacco pipe) and at his waist a *chakmak* (a lighter).

The Bharias purchase their clothes from the local weekly market. Their fashion in dress depends upon the quality and type of ready-to-wear dress brought and sold by the traders. Formerly their ancestors purchased cloth from the members of the *Katia* and *Mehra* castes, who made and traded in hand-loom clothes. The present generation uses mill-made cloth which is popular among the Bharias. According to the informants the clothes purchased from *Katia* and *Mehra* traders were cheaper durable. The mill-made clothes are good but costlier. In the former generation the children used a loin-cloth, *gopani* tucked through *badani* (a narrow strip of cloth passed between the legs and tied to a string tied round the waist). Now they love to wear *pajji* or *chhadi* (half-pants or underwears). Recently the Bharias have started using chappals made of unserviceable motor tyres. Each pair costs between Re. 1 and Rs. 2. They put on their best clothes when they go out for marketing or to a fair. The young boys of the present generation do not like to wear a dress made from coarse cloth; they desire to wear garments made of fine cloth. Thus the attitude towards dress has obviously undergone change among children although the elderly persons still insist on their children to wear the traditional dress.

A Bharia generally wears ornaments like *bakoda chuda*, *murkhi* and *chhalla*, all made of bronze or silver. *Bakoda* is a bangle used on the fore-arm, *chuda* on the wrist, *murkhi* on the ears and *chhalla* as rings. A few prosperous Bharias wear a necklace of silver called *sariya*. They claim that they are not much fond of ornaments but almost all the Bharias wear *chuda* made of a cheap metal.

Female dress: In former generations women wore rough hand-loom *saris*, and a few ornaments of simple design. Their *saris* were short in length. The present generation of Bharia women wear "mill-made clothes." The length of the *sari* varies from 12 to 18 feet. They wear *saris* in the same fashion as Gond women of the neighbourhood and also put on *polaka* (blouse) to cover their body. Munni, wife of Mehtar Bharia said that she disliked rough *saris*. The blue *saris* which she was wearing on the date of interview was purchased by her for Rs. 20 from the Chhindi market. Bharia women aspire to wear *saris* of good quality.

In the present generation the necklace, of rupee or fifty-paise coins strung in a thin silver chain, is rarely seen as an ornament among the Bharia women. This ornament has been replaced by *saria*, a necklace of silver. The young girls like to wear necklaces of attractive and shining beads called *pot*. Instead of wearing *karanphul* they now like to wear long ear-rings. They also like to wear silver *kakna*, *guletha* and *toda* on arms, which were used in former days. Recently they have also started wearing glass bangles. The practice of wearing lac bangles and heavy ornaments of cheaper metals is no more acceptable to Bharia girls. Instead, in each foot they wear *pehdi*. The social significance of wearing *pehdi* is the same as that of *pagri* by men. The married women must wear *pehdi*. On the death of the husband the pair of *pehdi* is removed. A widow cannot wear *pehdi* as it is a symbol of *suhag* or married status. Nowadays young Bharia women put on a small flower-like nose ornament, called *laong*. Finger rings studded with cheap coloured stones are also popular among the girls. Thus, it may be seen that the number of ornaments used has increased, obviously due to the influence of a nearby market. A large number of Bharia women visit the weekly market at Chhindi and are attracted by the glittering ornaments of attractive designs.

The hair style among the Bharia women has also undergone considerable change. In the former days the women made a bunch of hair and tied it with a thread called *chhawari*.

Nowadays they plait the hair and tie the tips with multicoloured cloth ribbons. Locally, plaiting is called *sakiya*. The girls now use hair-clips called *biranchi*. The change in female dress appears to be very fast especially in the quality of fabric and variety of designs.

Tattooing

Bharia women of the present generation are also fond of tattooing their bodies. For this they seek the help of a woman professional, who goes from house to house. She charges anything between Re. 1 and Rs. 3 according to the type of tattooing undertaken. She may also be paid for her services in kind, like grain. Tattooing is done on the forehead, on the arms and on the legs. A Bharia girl is first tattooed, when she is only a child, on the forehead and on the temples. The tattooing "ink" is prepared from the juice of the *bhilawan* tree. The skin is pricked with a needle and the tattooing-ink rubbed into the prick-holes. Though it is a painful operation, they say they have to undergo it because of the custom prevalent among them—*godana hamara jati rivaj hai* as they put it. They also believe that tattoo marks beautify their body. The girls and women look forward for the attractive designs of tattooing and crave for such body decoration.

Food and drink

A Bharia takes only one full meal a day. In the morning he takes *peja* or *mahua laddus*. He takes his full meal only in the evening after return from work. The dinner menu consists of rice or *kodo* or *kutki* or chappati made of maize or mango-seed flour. Wheat or *jowar* is used by only well-to-do Bharia families and is not included in their daily menu, being a costly item. They cook vegetables brought from forest or grown in their kitchen gardens. They use milk for preparing *ghee* as it fetches them good money. They instead of drinking milk, take buttermilk. They are fond of fish and take it after boiling and adding salt and chilly to it. Little edible oil is used by the Bharias as it is very costly for them. They also drink locally distilled *mahua* liquor prepared secretly, as they are afraid of Excise officials. Men and women love liquor and share it during festivals and after the *mahua* harvest.

The diet of Bharias has also undergone change due to their permanent settlement on land. Now they grow in their fields cereals like wheat and *jowar*, and pulses like *tuar*. In their kitchen gardens or *bari* they grow a few vegetables.

Vegetables

From the forest they bring vegetables like *dobhai bhaji*; *pipar bhaji*; *kular bhaji*; *pushti bhaji* (all leaves); *kand*; *karil* (bamboo roots), *biroli*, etc. During summer they collect *mahua* flowers and mangoes. A few grocery articles like jaggery, salt and chillies are purchased from the local weekly market.

Formerly they met their food requirements from forest and from *dahiya* cultivation fields but now they get them from the following three main sources: agricultural fields, kitchen garden and forest. Their weekly visits to the local markets have also influenced their eating habits and they sometimes enjoy oil-fried edibles with a cup of tea.

REFERENCE

1. Russell and Hiralal op. cit. 249.

3

ECONOMIC LIFE

AGRICULTURE continues to be the main economic activity of the Bharia tribe. From time immemorial agriculture had been supplemented with income from dairy farming. Collection of minor forest produce, fishing and daily wage earning are some of the subsidiary calls they attend to. Russell and Hiralal[1] have the following to say about the occupation of the tribe. "The Bharias are usually farm servants and field labourers and their services in these capacities are in much request. They are hardy and industrious, and so simple that it is an easy matter for their masters to involve them in perpetual debt, and thus to keep them bound to service from generation to generation. They have no understanding of accounts and the saying, 'pay for the marriage of a Bharia and he is your bond slave for ever,' sufficiently explains the methods adopted by their employers and creditors."

Dahiya cultivation

The main occupation of the Bharias since time immemorial has been *Dahiya* or slash-and-burn cultivation. In 1954 the Government of Madhya Pradesh banned this type of cultivation. Since then they have left with no alternative, taken to settled cultivation. The switchover from *dahiya* to settled cultivation was not a new phenomenon to the Bharia. He knew the Gonds of his neighbourhood engaged in settled cultivation. Even in Patalkot there were some Gonds and Bharias who had taken to settled cultivation. All the same, change from shifting to settled cultivation at one stroke brought anxiety and uneasiness among the Bharias. During the *dahiya* cultivation they celebrated *bidri*, worship of *Bhimsen* (this has continued). New methods of cultivation involved tools, particularly purchase of bullocks, for which a Bharia had little or no provision. But at the same time he feared the petty officials of the Forest and Revenue Departments and it was only under pressure that he adopted the new system. Nevertheless many Bharias continued to practise *dahiya* for some years untill 1965 when some of them were caught and produced before a Forest Officer at Parasia. They were released after a warning, but the minor forest officials continued to harass them on the plea that they should pay a fine of Rs 50 each. Thus, 1965 has been a turning point in the life of the Bharia as settled cultivation began to be practised by all Bharias, a change brought about for betterment through legislation.

The Bharias and Gonds call shifting cultivation *dahiya*; the Baigas of Mandla call it *bewar*; the Marias of Baster call it *penda* (shifting cultivation is known by different names among different tribes). The origin of this form of cultivation can be traced back to the days when the nomadic and pastoral tribes resorted to raising of crops through the most primitive methods. It represents the primitive man's first efforts to harness nature's gifts. The Bharias preferred this type of cultivation for more than one reason; they believed that the use of plough would amount to tearing the breast of the mother earth. *Dahiya*, on the other hand, did not require the use of bullocks; and, thirdly, it involved lesser human labour. *Dahiya* cultivation was permitted to be practised by the Bharias under the old system of *jagirdari* in which the *jagirdar* (landlord) received Rs. 2 to Rs. 4 "per axe annually" (an axe representing approximately one acre of land). For *dahiya* cultivation a part of the forest with fairly good growth of trees and bushes was selected during January-February. On one of the auspicious days, preferably a Monday, trees are felled by the male members of the family. The women usually clear the bushes with sickles after the trees had been felled. For a few weeks the felled vegetation is left to dry. Then in the months of May-June, the Bharias set fire to the dried trees and the ashes spread. Sowing of seeds was done immediately at the first shower of rains. The village *Bhumka* was consulted and the seeds broadcast at the rate of one standard measure (one *payali*) of seeds in a plot of about an acre.

Once the seeds are sown, the only activity left is weeding and protecting of the fields from monkeys and birds. The *bewar-kutki*, *madia*, *kang*, maize and beans are the main crops in the *dahiya* which ripen by October and are then reaped.

Today, when the Bharias look back and remember the abundant yields of crops they got from the *dahiya* fields they feel miserable. Indeed Premlal Bharia who, taking advantage of a landslide near his house, grew *dahiya* crops in that patch in 1971 produced a few ears of *kutki* and invited my attention to the rich yield he got. *Dahiya* is still cherished and the settled cultivation is said to have made them miserable, since due to poor soil and lack of irrigation more human energy is spent for declining yields.

Without any prejudice to the Bharias, however, *dahiya* was banned by the Government due to the national policy of protecting the forest which helped to arrest soil erosion and attracted rains.

Settled agriculture

In the Patalkot valley three categories of land can be identified: forest land, barren land, and cultivable land. Forest land is covered with forests and jungle-bush. Most of it is virgin and is being exploited for timber. Then there are certain tracts of barrenland spread with *moram*, pebbles and clay soil, on which only a few plants may be seen growing here and there. The land in the third category, that is, cultivable land can be grouped as under:

(i) *Barra* — This land has been under cultivation as *dahiya* fields.

(ii) *Kast* — This is agricultural land.

(iii) *Bari* About an acre of land is fenced by the villagers around their dwellings and vegetables are grown there. Sometimes they grow wheat, gram and maize also in these kitchen gardens known as *baris*.

Soil in the valley is poor; consisting, by and large, of sandy soil mixed with pebbles. Red yellow soil, *mutbarra* and thin variety soil, and *barra* are commonly seen. Loamy black soil, *moranel* and black soil or *kali jamun* are considered best suited for cultivation.

Whatever land a Bharia cultivated formerly was eventually granted to him under an ownership right called *Patta* by the overnment. The rights of cultivation given under the *jagirdars* have thus ceased. It may be pointed out that each Bharia cultivator had a *bahi* in which the record of land was mentioned during the *jagirdari* days, and it was on the basis of *bahi* that the Bharias were granted individual *Patta* title.

The Bharias now distinguish two types of fields, *bari* (kitchen garden) and *khet* (field), though both are worked with a *bakhar* only. Those parts of *bari* in which wheat and gram are sown are abundantly manured and ploughed. Since the soil is shallow and stony, it is advantageous to turn it only lightly.

Cropping pattern

Kharif is the main crop raised by the Bharias and they grow in this season *kutki*, maize and some *jowar*. Sowing is done in June-July and harvesting in October-November. These crops are grown on any soil and do not require intensive ploughing. Rabi crops (wheat and gram) are sown in winter, as already said mostly in their *baris* during December-January. They harvest these crops after Holi, in April-May. They do not put sufficient manure in the fields with the result that the yields are often poor. The Bharias, instead of keeping wheat and gram for their consumption, sell them in the market and in return purchase millets, salt, tobacco, cloth and other requirements. In their *baris*, the Bharias also grow maize and such vegetables as pumpkin, brinjal, tomatoes, chillies, turmeric, beans and occassionally tobacco.

Agricultural operation

Manuring: The *baris* and fields in lowlands are usually manured once before the rains and, at times, after the rains, when wheat crop is to be sown. Cow-dung is the only manure used by the Bharias. The fields of *kodo-kutki* are never manured.

Ploughing: For ploughing the Kharif fields Bharias use a *bakhar* in the beginning of July after performing the *Bidri* rite. They plough the fields at least twice before sowing.

Sowing: With the help of a bamboo basket the seeds are broadcast in the fields and the soil slightly turned up with *bakhar*.

Fencing: The Rabi fields are fenced with bamboo and wood to protect the crops from wild animals and cattle but the Kharif fields are left unfenced.

Weeding: The women are deployed at least twice for weeding out the undesirable growth from the Kharif fields.

Watching: During daytime women and children watch the crops to keep away stray cattle and other wild animals. During the night men may keep a watch. Wild animals such as sambhar and monkeys are a menance to the crops in Patalkot. The Bharias, however, seem to have a great faith in *Bhimsen* who is believed to protect the crops at all times against any heavy damage.

Harvesting, threshing and winnowing

After harvesting of *kodo-kutki* with sickles, threshing is done either in the fields or in their houses with the help of a few bullocks or sometimes by the family members themselves with their feet. The husk is removed with the help of *supa* (winnowing fan).

Storing

Grains are usually measured in *payalis* (a local measure) after the same have been brought home, and are stored in the *kothis* made of mud and husk. Maize 'heads' are usually hung on the poles erected outside the house in a conical fashion.

Subsidiary economic activities

Forest produce: Except in some cases, no Bharia is able to produce enough grains for the family's annual consumption. Indeed the low yields from the fields compel most of them to supplement subsistence through other means like collection of forest produce. In the month of *Phalgun* and *Chaitra* (March-April) almost all Bharias engage themselves in the collection of *mahua* flowers. Except the old, the children, and the infirm, all able-bodied persons go to live by the *mahua* trees. Children usually bring food from home but in some cases the husband and wife may even make their cooking arrangements near the trees. Each family has its own trees and in the flowering season these are fenced with thorns to prevent monkeys from coming near them.

The collected flowers are sent home for drying and storing. Many days' exposure to sunlight is essential for preserving the flowers. *Mahua* flowers may be eaten fresh, but large quantities are used for preparing liquor during the *mahua* season. The dried flowers are also ground, mixed with water and made into gruel. Some Bharias while going to work as labourers, carry *laddus* (cake) balls made of *mahua* flowers.

Apart from *mahua* flowers, the Bharias collect mangoes (especially mango seeds). The mango seeds are ground into flour, after these have been washed and dried, and are made into a kind of dough to be baked as bread. In times of shortage, and also to save food for the lean season, the Bharias eat bread of mango seeds in large quantities to supplement their food.

Another forest produce they collect is *achar* or what is called *chironji* (a kind of wild mango). The fruits are eaten and the nuts washed to yield *chironji*, after they have been dried. The hard working Bharias sit down and break each small nut before they can take it to the Chhindi market for sale to merchants. The forest also yields roots, tubers and honey. Honey is an item which is in great demand and they collect the same by driving away the flies with the help of fire, and then reach up to the hive to remove it. Bharias also collect certain grasses and make brooms out of them to be sold to contractors in the Chhindi market. Sometimes they collect *awala* (gooseberry) which they sell to merchants.

Hunting

Hunting is no more an economic pursuit for the Bharias at present. In the past when the valley was full of forests, it is reported that they did hunting as part of their food collection effort. Spears, axes and bows and arrows were the principal weapons used for hunting. But hunting as part of their culture has ceased to be recognised as is clear from the fact that there is not even the ritual hunting after the *Bidri* rite which, among some of the tribes, had been significant until recently when the rules of the Forest Department were amended restricting destruction of animal life. Wild pigs are said to damage the standing crops sometimes, but they prefer to call a *shikari* (hunter) from among the Gonds who owns a gun to kill the pigs. However, they admitted that they sometimes encircled an animal, and made it jump into a ravine. If a sambhar, for example, was killed in this manner, they divided the flesh and ate the venison with avidity.

Fishing

Fishing is comparatively more important to the Bharias and they can be regarded as good fishermen. They use a few well-known methods of fishing. Some of them make use of conical traps made of bamboo, but this method has become obsolete during the past few decades. By far the most important method is by poisoning. They bring roots of *khummi* tree or bark of *sarai* or *gural* tree and pound them to extract its juice. The flow of the water of the river is arrested by erecting a low bund with mud and stones and the juice is thrown in the water. After a while, the fish become blind, they say under the effect of the juice, and then collect them. The other method is called *ulcha.* In this they arrest the flow of the river and bale out water with metal plates into the main stream of the river. When little water is left, fish become visible and can be caught with hands or with the help of traps.

Fish adds to the protein requirement of the Bharia, and when the young men and women have little or nothing to do at home or in the field, they go for fishing to provide food and good pastime. They return in the afternoon after sharing the catch, if members of more than one family join in the venture. Otherwise the family brings its own catch which may be half to one kilogram of fish. The fish are of small variety; nevertheless the catch brings a change in the routine food of the Bharia. Fish are rarely sold to others and in many cases they are scorched in fire and eaten near the river itself, leaving a small part for the members of the family.

Cattle breeding and dairy farming

Cattle breeding is an ancillary activity to agriculture but far more important than fishing and collection of forest produce. The cattle strength of 24 Bharia families revealed that they had 116 cows, 31 buffaloes, 9 goats and 81 bullocks. The main object of cattle-rearing is for milk and milk products. *Ghee* (clarified butter) is collected and sold to shop-keepers at Rs. 8 to Rs. 12 per kilogram depending upon the season. The *chhanch* (butter milk) is part of the Bharia diet. However, while the Bharias have had the tradition of rearing cattle, it appears that they did not care to milk their cows in the past, as they believed that this affects the health of the calves. The calves in those days were allowed to suckle the milk freely and grew strong. But for the past three decades or so practically all of them have begun to milk their cows.

In general, the quality of the Bharia cattle is good. The animals fatten during the rains when the grazing grounds become rich with green lush grass, but they grow weak during the summer. The cattle are looked after by the Bharia graziers who may charge 50 paise for a cow and one rupee for a buffalo per month. Those Bharias who have grown-up children take care of the cattle themselves.

When a calf grows into a young bull, the Bharias train it up for ploughing. They yoke it with a bullock, and sometimes even with a trained cow, a practice which is rather uncommon. And the young bull, first unyielding, gradually learns what is expected of it. They get the bull castrated and put a thin rope through its nose as is done in the plains. The Bharias while training the bullock encourage it to draw the plough by singing: *Tu dharti ka putra re, chal beta chal*, meaning move son, move: you are the son of the earth. The practice of using bullocks for ploughing, castrating them, etc., have come only after settled cultivation, and was not there during *dahiya* cultivation.

A full-grown bullock may cost anything between Rs 150 and Rs 250 and for this reason the Bharias prefer to raise their own bullocks. Many of them, however, do not own any bullock. Those who own no land are called *thelua*. They have to work mostly as labourers on the farms of others or seek labour under the forest contractors.

Poultry

The Bharias also rear fowl and there would be few families who have no birds. The poultry are not large. Each family may have one or two birds, occasionally more, at any one time. In the 24 families surveyed there were 37 birds. Some of them said that since the birds had died due to disease they had not brought new birds, but that should not mean that they would not rear fowls.

The fowls find a place in the *bari* or they may hide in the corners of the house during the night. However, they are always provided with baskets, when they lay eggs.

Fowls are necessary for rituals, but the Bharias ordinarily rear them for the eggs which sometimes they eat or sell for making purchases of their daily requirements. Others may allow the eggs to be hatched so as to increase the poultry. The birds are *deshi* or of ordinary variety and are able to thrive well, though sometimes *Ranikhet* disease takes a heavy toll of them.

Labour

The Bharias are unskilled labourers and find employment of two types: (a) on farms and in forests and (b) as wage earners in road and building construction. They prefer to work as farm labourers for the simple reason that the payment is usually in grains. When a Gond or a well-to-do Bharia engages them for work on his fields, he usually pays about two *payalis* (about two kilograms) of grain—*kodo* or *kutki* per day per person. At other times they have to seek employment under forest contractors. In terms of money, the payment is Rs. 1.50 per day for men and Rs 1.25 for women. The contractors who receive forest coupes for extraction of timber have to make their own arrangements for bringing the transport vehicle deep into the forest, which involves laying of rough roads. The Bharia labourers have thus been able to connect the forests of Rated, Jad and Mandal with fair-weather roads and the money so earned has helped them to improve their economic condition. The contractors also engage them for felling trees, for removing and stacking of wood and for loading of timber and unloading it from lorries. They also engage the Bharias for making charcoal. Nowadays, on an average, two members of each house-hold have to work as labourers for four to six months in a year to make their living. Clearly then, on the one hand, roads built to reach the interior of Patalkot have aroused the valley from its age-old slumber, on the other the Bharias are able to get adequate employment under the Forest Department and their contractors. In 1971 they worked as labourers for carriyng cement bags from the top of the *kot* (hill) to the site of the new school building under construction. They were being paid Re 1 for transporting three bags which they were able to do in about three hours. As far as possible, the Bharias do not like to go out of their valley to seek employment and they were keen that the government should repair the flight of steps which had been washed off. This, they said, would afford them adequate employment for some months.

Daily round of economic activity

It is only proper that the Bharias whose economy is still at the subsistence level should be hard working. Indeed they hardly have any "leisure time." For this reason it is difficult to meet a Bharia during the day, and certainly he has no time to respond to any detailed inquiries. He does not like to stay at home except when there are some festivities, or he is ill.

Both men and women work hard and the work is patterned according to the season and the agricultural activity awaiting completion. It would be clear from the calendar of agricultural operations that *Magh* and *Phalgun* (January-February) are the only months in which they get some respite from work. And this is the time when he must work as a labourer. At other times during the year, when he has less work in the fields, he collects, depending upon the season, *mahua* flowers or mango stones or goes for fishing in the river, if jobs cannot be found. But nowadays, except during the rains, jobs are available with comparative ease due to increased forest exploitation.

Let us, however, briefly review the average daily economic activities of both sexes. The Bharia woman gets up rather early and the first thing she does is to kindle a fire in the hearth, if it is not already there. Then the day's cooking begins and what is cooked naturally depends upon the season. One may, during the *mahua* season, for example, cook *mahua* for both the meals except when a break from the routine becomes essential. This done, she sweeps the house, fetches water (she may send her daughter to do so) and serves the food to the family to enable them to get ready for the day's toil.

However, if there is no flour for making *chappatis*, she would first grind cereals. If one were to stay in a Bharia village, one may hear the rattling sound of grinding stones coming from several houses in the early morning. There is, however, no hard and fast rule, many women grind cereals in the evenings.

Once the food—it may be only *pej* which is a gruel of maize or *jowar* flower—is ready, the husband gets up and after a wash eats the food (or drinks the *pej*). This done he gets ready for his fields, or for the forest. If he is to go as a labourer, he must hurry to be in time with others.

The housewife feeds the children who then sit or play with other children. After this she also eats, if not already done with the children, and begins the domestic chores. There is so much to be done: the cowshed is to be cleaned; the cowdung is to be collected at one place; a coating of cowdung on the floor is probably necessary; the grains are to be pounded before grinding, and so on. All this work is scheduled to be done sometime or the other during the day and she must time it according to her convenience, except that the cowshed must be cleaned in the morning.

In the *bari* she may be required to spread the cowdung, or she may be required to go for weeding her fields. If the day's work required her to be out in the fields she leaves the house unlocked, leaving it to the care of small children. When the mother leaves home, the younger children might cry, but she does not wait or stay on. Unless she is guarding the *bari* near her house, she must ensure that she returns in good time, before afternoon to feed the children. Yet in the peak season of agriculture she might take them along to the field so that she might continue her work in the field till late in the evening. On return in the evening, the supper is cooked. The husband returns home and the family sits together to eat the evening meal. It is only then that the men get some time to relax. Someone may drop in and then they may gossip and share a *chilam*. They all go to sleep early.

Division of labour

The Bharia men do the arduous and tough tasks themselves and leave the monotonous and comparatively light work to their women. Sometimes magico-religious rites also govern the division of labour between them. Women are forbidden to take up those tasks which require climbing up the roof or trees. They are also tabooed to operate the plough. Traditionally the Bharia women have been exempted from sowing and threshing operations. Household duties such as preparing food, fetching water, taking care of children, washing clothes are performed by them. Customarily they are not sent to watch the crops in the fields during night. The Bharia men take up ploughing, digging and other jobs involving hard work in the fields. They repair the agricultural implements and take the cattle out of the sheds in the mornings. Threshing and winnowing of grains are assigned to men with only a little assistance from their women. It is mostly men who go for casual labour, though unmarried girls or women who have left their husbands also freely seek employment. The Bharias do not like their married women to undertake work outside. Again the men collect honey, indigenous medicines, herbs, etc. They go for fishing and during leisure they make ropes. The women help the family by gathering *mahua* flowers, mangoes and *harra* and rear poultry.

Social and religious functions are performed by both the sexes. Men and women both visit their relatives and friends, attend marriages and mournings but only men participate in the meetings of the Panchayat. Performing various religious ceremonies is also the prerogative of men. The women, on the other hand, may visit the female friends and take part in the recreational activities of the village. With regard to miscellaneous jobs the men also attend to the officers and do *begar* (odd jobs) for them. In other activities men and women equally share the workload. With the change of times the Bharia women have started going to the weekly markets and it is they who select the commodities of their choice for household consumption.

Inter-family economic co-operation

The Bharias appear to be an individualistic tribe among whom there is remarkable lack of inter-family co-operation in economic activities. One does not find mutual help being extended to each other in agricultural operations. Each family is supposed to work on its own and should it need help requisite manpower must be engaged on payment. Even among brothers there is lack of co-operation in farming activities. The only instance of some sort of co-operation visible in this community is that when the father-in-law so wishes, he may request his daughter and son-in-law to help him, and in return they may receive some presents and or help at the time of harvesting.

Inter-community economic interaction

The Bharias, as mentioned in the chapter on religion, celebrate the *Bidri* rite jointly with the Gonds. But beyond this, the two communities do not interact economically. The Bharias, though poor, rarely go to the Gonds asking for a loan. On the other hand they work on the fields of the Gonds and earn wages, which to some extent results in interaction between the two communities.

The main economic interaction of the Bharias with other communities is found in the market at Chhindi which both men and women frequently visit.

While the Bharias produce or procure almost everything they need for their subsistence there are certain other things which they need in their daily life, such as earthen pots, salt, spices, kerosene oil, tobacco, jaggery, bangles, ornaments, clothes (including ready-made garments) and other trinkets. These are available on the market day at Chhindi. And it is in the market where they sometimes afford to relish some sweets, *pan* and tea. Among the important items for sale or barter by the Bharias are small quantities of wheat, gram, *chironji*, *ghee*, eggs, hand-made ropes, brooms and honey. *Ghee* is in great demand and the merchants usually wait a mile away from the market and buy it off before it reaches the market. Both barter and cash transactions are in vogue in the market.

The shops in Chhindi are of two kinds. Some of them, mostly owned by Muslims, are permanent and are open on all days. Others are of temporary nature. Petty shopkeepers and vendors bring their wares such as clothes, jaggery, tobacco, etc., on the market day from 15 to 20 miles or even more, either on horse-back or in bullock-carts. On arrival, they sit in their fixed places with their wares arranged properly. Once a Bharia reaches his usual "merchant friend" the latter measures his grains and immediately asks for his requirements. If he has nothing to purchase from his wares, he gives the money to enable him to purchase his requirements from another shop. In the process, the Bharia may or may not always get cheated, but usually he is not a good bargainer and pays more for a thing than the prevailing price.

The Bharias prefer to make purchases straightaway, without much thought of checking the price. They mentally fix a price which they can offer, and quote it to the shopkeeper, and the shopkeeper once he sees his need he gets the price he wants by convincing him in several ways.

Young Bharia women meet their friends in the bazar and they often go about together to purchase trinkets, scented oils and other alluring objects. It is the market which decides their fashion, change in the colour or borders of saris or cloth and colour of the blouse. Indeed much has changed in the dress during the past two decades, and there is a visible change in the ornaments too.

The market at Chhindi has been in existence for over 60 or 70 years, if not more, and it is the one important agent of social change among the Bharias. It is not only a centre of redistribution of economic resources of the region but also a centre of social, religious and political activity of the tribes and castes of the region.[2]

Economic trends

Income: A couple of decades ago only a few families undertook farm work and the rest depended on agriculture and other subsidiary sources; about half of the families took to cattle rearing. At present, however, families engaged in farm labour have increased to more than half and those in agriculture declined to a little more than a quarter and only a few families are engaged in cattle rearing. Previously poultry was meant for self-consumption only and cattle were sold for meeting the expenses of marriage, feast or litigation. A bullock was sold then for Rs 80 and a cow for Rs 40. This is done even now but the prices have increased and so those who own cattle are better off. Rope-making is the popular cottage industry with the Bharias. By selling *deo bahari*, a kind of broom, a family may earn up to Rs 5 or more a month. Collection of minor forest produce and working as farm labour are other sources of income, and they are better off now than they were a couple of decades back.

A Bharia earns more than half of his total income by working as a labourer. His other sources are agriculture and sale of *ghee*, poultry, brooms, ropes, etc. Annual average income of a Bharia household is approximately Rs 700.

Expenditure: The maximum expenditure (70 to 85 per cent) is on food. The Bharias' main food items are *kodo* and *kutki* which they grow in their fields. Meat, fish, roots and fruits are procured from the jungles. They use their earnings from subsidiary sources for purchasing clothes, fuel and kerosene oil, etc. The per capita annual expenditure on clothing is about Rs 10, and a family spends about Rs 50 annually on liquor. A good part of the earnings is used on social ceremonies whenever performed. Nevertheless the Bharia does not believe in borrowing, a habit unlike that of the neighbouring Gonds. He has little or no savings.

Ownership of property: Right to own land is acquired by the Bharias according to any of the following methods: 1. inheritance, 2. first cultivation, 3. by purchasing cultivation rights.

Those who own land have full rights. They can sell, mortgage, share or give it to anyone on a rental basis. Trees on their land are their property.

Now the Bharias can transfer their land to non-tribals only after seeking the approval of the Collector. Chhindwara, as per a Government directive, under which transfer of land to non-tr ibals by tribals is controlled.

Personal property comprises lands, house, utensils, clothes, ornaments and cattle. The property is inherited by the sons equally. When girls are given away in marriage they receive some ornaments and utensils. Ornaments remain their property and, except with their consent, the husbands cannot dispose them.

REFERENCES AND NOTES

1. Russel and Hira Lal, op. cit. p. 250.
2. Sinha, D. P., *Culture change in an Intertribal Market*, London, 1968, p. 101.

4

SOCIAL STRUCTURE

THE SOCIAL structure of the Bharia tribe is characterised by a set of relationships that exist among the members of the group at various levels within the framework of different social units. The important units involved in the social structure are the family, the kin groups, the clan and the village community. An appreciation of the social organisation of the Bharias, therefore, requires a study of the social relationships.

The family

Composition and type: As in any other society, family is the basic social unit among the Bharias which is identified by the procreative role, a common residence, economic co-operation and mutual protection. A family generally includes the husband, wife and their unmarried children forming a nuclear unit. Occasionally, however, certain close relations may also be added to the primary family group, thus making it an extended family. This may happen in several ways. At times a father, who has no grown-up son to share his burden, may like to have his son-in-law, if he has a daughter, to stay with him. More often this arrangement may be the result of the son-in-law working as a *lamjhana* (marriage by service. The person undergoing this is also known by the same term) before the girl is married to him. It may also happen that the married sons may not separate from family of orientation immediately after marriage: in many cases they

TABLE. 3: **Composition and type of family**

Name of head of family	Name of village	Ego and relationship of members to him in the family	Total	Whether Nuclear* (N) or Extended (E)
Nanhi	Rated	Ego, Wi, Dau, 4 So	7	N
Mehtar	-do-	Ego, Wi, 3 Dau, 2So	7	N
Chappu	-do-	Ego, Wi, So, 2Dau, Wi So from previous husband	6	E
Premlal	-do-	Ego, Wi, 2So, SoWi, 3SoSo	8	E
Kaaloo	-do-	Ego, Wi, So, SoWi, SoSo, SoWimo	6	E
Pasu	-do-	Ego, Wi, 5So, E1So WiSoSo	9	E
Jangal Singh	-do-	Ego, Wi, 2So, Dau, Bro.	6	E
Halku	-do-	Ego, Wi, 3So, 2So Wi, 3SoSo, 3 So Dau	13	E
Jeevan	-do-	Ego, 2Wi, Dau, would be son-in-law or Lamjhana	5	E
Gothal	-do-	Ego, Wi, Dau	3	N
Basodi	-do-	Ego, Wi, So, 2Dau	5	N
Nagar	-do-	Ego, Wi, 4So	6	N
Hori	-do-	Ego, Wi, So, 2 Dau	5	N
Chintaman	-do-	Ego, Wi, Dau, So & a Lamjhana	5	E
Simiyari	-do-	Ego, Wi, 3So, 3 Dau	8	N
Shondal	-do-	Ego, 2Wi, 2So, Dau, Son-in-law	7	E
Shankar	-do-	Ego, Wi, 2 So	4	N
Chamru	Dudipatha	Ego, Wi, So	3	N
Potal	-do-	Ego, Wi, So, 4 Dau	7	N
Jugru	-do-	Ego, Wi, Ego's Fa, & Mo, 2So, 5 Dau, Ego's Wife's Dau from previous husband	12	E
Dhende	-do-	Ego, Wi, 6So	8	N
Najaroo	-do-	Ego, Wi, 2 Br, 2 Br Wi	6	E
Budhan	-do-	Ego, Wi	2	N
Jatru	-do-	Ego, Wi	2	N
			150	

*For the purpose of this study a nuclear family is one with the husband, wife and unmarried children and if this nucleus is extended by the other closely related kins, then it is considered as an extended family. The data pertains to 1976.

continue to live with their wives and children. Occasionally, though the incidence may be rare, a widowed mother-in-law, who has none to support her, may come with her children to live with her son-in-law. Thus, side by side with the nuclear family, there also exists extended family system among the Bharias, a condition brought about more by compulsion than the norm.

Within the confines of the Patalkot valley there are in all 91 Bharia families living in different villages. Of these 24 families of Rated and Daudipatha villages were studied to find out the composition and type of family of the Bharias living there as detailed in Table 3.

Out of the 24 families enumerated, 13 were nuclear and the remaining 11 were extended. Nuclear family, it would be seen, appears to be the general norm in the Bharia society although, presence of extended families is also almost equally strong.

The extended families among the Bharias can be grouped under four broad categories according to their composition. These are: (i) ego, his wife and married sons with their spouses and children; (ii) ego and his brother, the former's wife and children; (iii) ego, wife, children and son-in-law; and (iv) others. The first, third and fourth categories account for three cases each whereas category (ii) accounts for two cases. The phenomenon presented above gives an indication of the trend of the types of families prevalent among the Bharias.

Size of family

The Bharias prefer a large family. The study, showed that the average number of members in a family was 6.25 persons. The largest had 13 members and the smallest two. Percentage distribution of the number of members in a family is given in Table 4.

Thus it is clear that the majority (54.17 per cent) of the families have a large number of members ranging from six to nine. On the other side 8.33 per cent families have from 10 to 13 members. In other words, about 63 per cent of the families fall above the average number. This gives an indication of the preference of the Bharias for large families.

TABLE 4: **Percentage distribution according to the number of members in family**

No. of members	No. of families	Percentage distribution
2—	2	8.33
3 to 5	7	29.17
6 to 9	13	54.17
10 to 13	2	8.33
14+	—	—
Total	24	100.00

Functions of Bharia family

As in any other family, the essential functions of a Bharia family are procreative, productive and protective. The wife serves her husband, rears the children and gives exclusive privilege of sexual relations to her husband. The husband, on his part, remains faithful to his wife, protects the family and provides economic resources for the continuance of the group. A wife is as necessary to the man as man is to the wife.

Children are eagerly sought for, as they maintain the continuity of the family,lineage and the clan. They too co-operate with their parents in the latter's productive-cum-protective role. The anxiety of the Bharia for their children is revealed from the fact that during religious rites the Bharia priest prays not merely for the fertility of the land but also for the fertility of the woman and longevity of children.

Another fundamental function of the Bharia family is economic. The man and woman are considered by the Bharia as the two wheels of the same cart which must work together to carry forward the burden of the family. There are certain occupations and family chores which fall exclusively within the domain of the woman and others exclusively of the man. There are some common functions as well.

In the field of domestic chores, a woman fetches water,

sweeps and cleans the house, pounds and husks grains, grinds grain into flour, cooks food, cleans and sweeps the cattleshed and removes cowdung to the manure heap near the *bari*, rears the children, cooks and distributes food to the family and entertains the female guests. There is not much work for the man in these domestic chores, though he may help in rearing the children, fetching water during the illness of the wife and milking cows, repairing tools used in cultivation, looking after the cattle, entertaining male guests and repairing the house. These are the duties for men, but a few may do a little more to keep their wives happy. Man is primarily expected to do the outdoor duties. He must prepare fields by ploughing them, sow seeds and reap the harvest. Woman's work in agriculture is limited to spreading of manure, weeding and giving help in harvesting. The fact that until two generations ago, and in certain cases even now, it was for the man to open earthen containers for taking out grains and then close them himself, showed that he was the patriarch who controlled the food supply and was responsible for its storage, distribution and consumption.

Hunting has ceased now; community hunting which had been an essential feature in the past is not undertaken now even as a ritual. It was for the man to fish and the women could go to the river-side and fetch fish, as they sometimes do even now. But fishing as such is regarded as a manly occupation.

Care of the cattle, sale or transfer of cattle are entirely for the Bharia man and though the woman has her say she would not go against the decision of her husband who usually consults his kinsmen.

Finally, there are certain duties in relation to religious activities which are shared by man and woman. A wife may participate in the feast and in dances, but she does not go near those shrines where *Bhumka* and Bharia males alone can remain present. Among the Bharias of Patalkot, men alone can become a *Bhumka*, the tribal priest.

Another important function of the family is socialisation or education and training. Young children are educated in the cultural values and norms of the society, trained in the different roles to be played as a member of the society and their contribution in the economic pursuit.

Right from the tender age, female children are trained to look after the young ones, to manage a family, do cooking and the like. The boys, on the other hand, are trained to play the role in different economic pursuits of the family and in the protective function, etc. Parents narrate to the children tribal lores, myths and folk beliefs thus socialising the children to the society they belong to. The folk art, the folk songs and dances are learnt gradually by the time they reach adolescence. Girls join dancing parties first as beginners and later as regular participants. In the field of economic pursuits, at this time they start helping their parents in the collection of forest produce, agricultural activities, etc. It has been observed that one of the main reasons why tribals hesitate to send their children to school is because they become earning members of the family even in their childhood.

Kinship organisation

Individual families, in the Bharia society, are linked by ties either of lineage or of marriage. The lineage ties are widened to form the horizon of clan, the members of which include agnatic kins and are invariably identified by a common clan name. The second group originates from nuptial ties and thus the members of the contracting families create relationships of different categories. Intra-village marriages nourish interpersonal relations in the same village or locality.

Thus, residential kin groups and clan form the two important kinship organisations of the Bharia society. Whether inside the clan or not, common residence provides a fraternal feeling among the members making the residential kin-groups a well-knit social organisation.

Information from two villages regarding clan organisation in them shows that there is a concentration of one clan in one particular village. This tends to show that once uniclan villages prevailed among the Bharias. Today, however, the trend is towards multiclan villages as can be seen in the discussion on clan organisation.

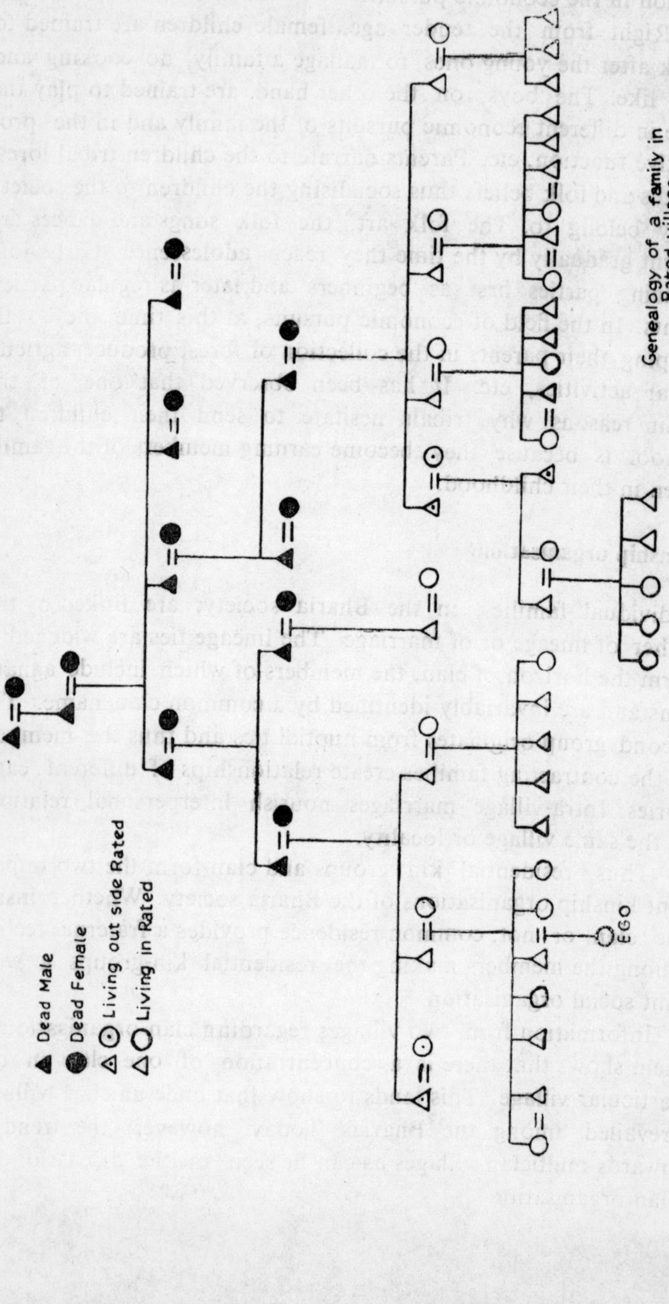

Genealogy of a family in Rated village.

It is seen that common residence is shared normally by the members of the same lineage. This is evident from the genealogy of a family in Rated village given in the chart on the facing page.

In the genealogy given here it may be seen that out of nine lineages seven share the same locality of residence. Two of them stay in the adjoining villages. But, all the nine lineages derive their origin from the same common ancestor, that is, *Phirangi*. It is clear that the residential kin groups are bound in most cases by common descent. In certain cases, however, families related to the *ego's* cognates may also come to stay. In other words the agnatic-cognatic relations normally bind the residents of the same village.

The ideal residential pattern of a patrilineage is shown in the sketch map given on the facing page. In this case heads of families are related to each other by close agnatic bonds.

These clan groups are always expected to help each other at the time of need and in daily life generally. In this group of agnates, Khuman and Chamru, though living in Chimtipur and Daudipatha, have equal importance, for they must be consulted before a decision is taken to marry off a girl, or to send a boy to work as *lamjhana*. On anything that affects the solidarity of this segment of agnates the senior members have got to be unanimous, or else there would be tendencies towards fission, which the Bharias think undesirable among immediate patrikin. The relations of other segments of patrikin with this segment are of less strength, and in many cases when they pass to the class of "very distant", that is, when the genealogical connection is forgotten, the entire unity may consider itself one only for the purpose of exogamy. The father of a girl, as for example, is expected to consult his patrikin before he settles her marriage. If he ignores any senior member of his patrilineage, it would be viewed as a serious lapse. Similarly, if the girl who, prior to her marriage, is expected to visit the house of her patrikin to "cry" according to Bharia custom, fails to visit them, it would be a serious lapse.The relations would be strained between the two, and in times to come if these are not mended they would create fission among the patrikin for the future. It may be mentioned

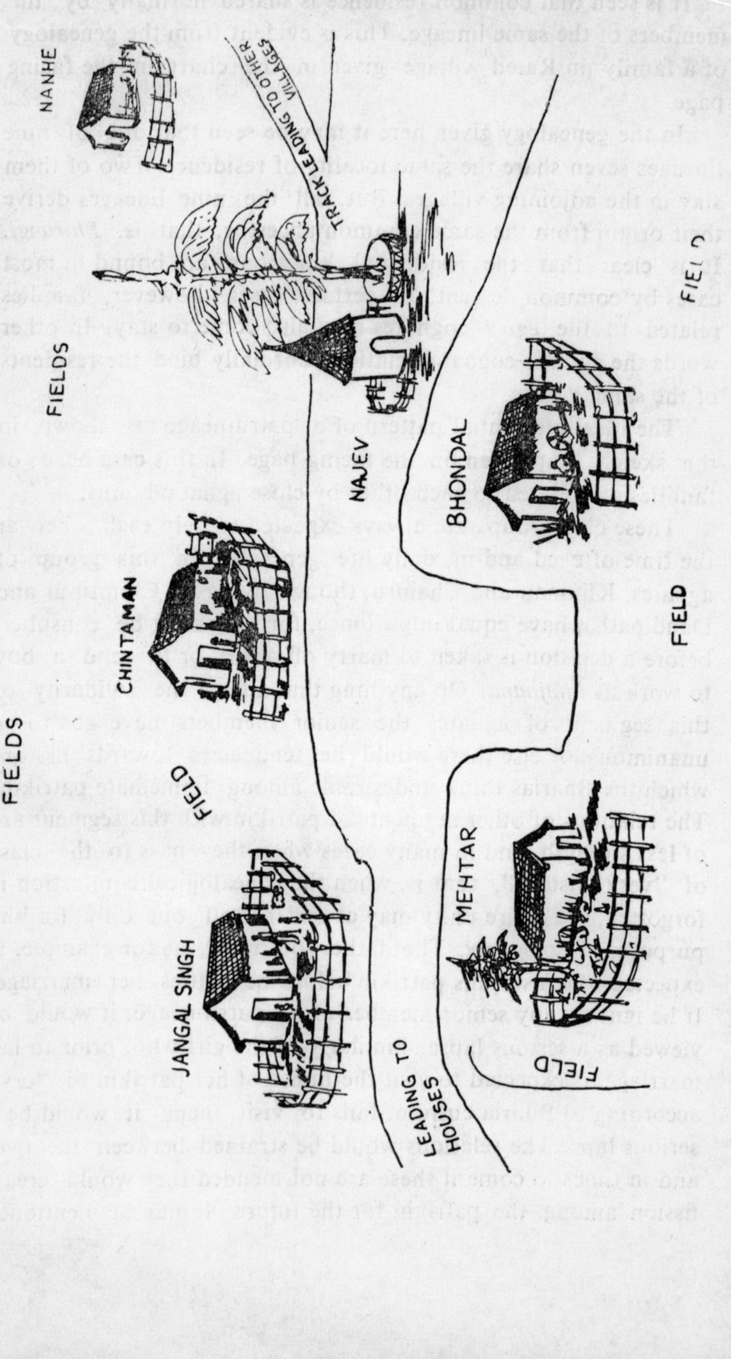
NANHE
TRACK LEADING TO OTHER VILLAGES
FIELDS
FIELD
NAJEV
BHONDAL
CHINTAMAN
FIELD
FIELDS
FIELD
MEHTAR
JANGAL SINGH
LEADING TO HOUSES
FIELD

here that there may be three or four such patrilineal segments of different clans living in the same village and that similar relations may obtain among the members of each of them.

It we take into account the fact that many marriages take place between the members of these different segments following, of course, the rules of clan exogamy and the prohibited degrees, it is easier to see the families of different segments furnishing a network of affinal relationships. We will touch upon these relationships later. Here what we see is that the various segments of different clans in a village are not watertight compartments but have inter-relationships which can be fully discovered if we probe into the individual marriages.

Kinship and lineage

The system of kinship plays an important role in all human societies and more so in the tribal societies in which the inter-personal relations, economic co-operation and a range of other social obligations between related individuals are largely governed by the rules of kinship. To make an analysis of the Bharia kinship system, let us first define the kinship terms and their range of application. The kinship terms are found to be classificatory and a kinship term covers, or is applied to, persons of more than one kinship category defined by age, sex and genealogical relationship as is seen in Table 5.

Turning to one's own generation in the patrigroup, we find that one addresses his brothers by the term *Bhaiya* (brother) and that he uses this term for the sons of his father's brothers. In the first ascending generation one addresses his father by the term *Dadda* and applies the same term for father's brothers who are senior in age to the father. The terms *Kakka* is used to cover the younger brothers of the father. The term is applied to all males of patrilineage of the father's generation who are junior to father in age and with whom relationship can be traced genealogically. In the Father's father's (grand father's) generation the term of address is *Aiya* of which another synonym given is *Baba*. The term *Baba* appears to be, however, "referential" than a term of address.

TABLE 5: **Kinship terms and categorization**

Kinship term	Category of relative	Term for reciprocation
Dadda	Fa	Beta (or Baiya)
	FaElBr	
Kakka	FaYoBr	Dau
	WiMoBr	
Baba or	FaFa	Aiya/Baba
Aiya	FaFaBr (El or Yo)	Aiya/Baba
	MoMoHu	Nana/Baba
	WiFaFa	Nati
	WiFaFaBr	Nati
Only Bhaiya	Br (El or Yo)	Bhaiya
Mama	MoBr	Mamu/Damad
	MoMoBr	Mamu/Damad
	WiFa	Mamu/Damad
	WiFaBr (El or Yo)	Mamu/Damad
	FaSisHu	Mamu/Damad
Mausia	WiFaSisHu	Beta/Bacha
	MoSisHu	
Samdhi	SisHu (Yo or El)	Samdhi
	WiBr (El)	
Dadi	WiBr (Yo)	Jeeja/Samdhi
Bhari	WiSisHu	Bhai (Ref. Sadhu)
Bau	Mo	
	MoSis (Yo)	Beta
	FaBrWi (El)	
Kaki	FaBrWi (Yo)	
	WiFaSis	
Mausi	MoSis (El)	
	WiFaSis	
Fua or	FaSis (El or Yo)	Damad
Mami	MoBrWi	
	WiMo	
	WiMoSis	
	WiFaBrWi	
Bahu	YoBrWi	(Ref. Jeth)
	SoWi	(Ref. Sasur)
Nani/	FaFaWi	
Aji	FaFaBrWi (El)	
	MoMo	
	MoMoSis	
	MoMoBrWi	
Jad Sas	WiSis (El)	Damad

Turning to the wives of these relatives we find that one uses two different terms for brothers' wives. The wives of senior brothers are addressed by the term *Bhabhi* but there is no term of address for wives of younger brothers. Indeed the *Jeth* (as the Ego would be referred to) is not expected to address them by name nor cultivate any familiarity with them. This is, indeed what may be expected, because should the father die the elder brother has to assume his responsibilities and must, therefore, be distinguished and respected. The Bharia women say that *Sasur* and *Jeth* are like *Bhagwan* or god and they are expected to give both of them the same respect.

In the father's generation one makes a distinction between the wife of father's elder brother who is addressed as *Bau* (mother) or *Badi Bau* (senior mother), and wife of father's younger brother who is addressed as *Kaki*. In the grand father's generation the grand mothers are addressed by the term *Bhabhi*. Bharias say that a grandfather may joke with the grand child. They say that the grand parents and grand children stand in a sort of joking relationship or *hansikarista*. Any generation above that of grandfather is regarded the same as that of grandfather. This shows that the Bharia essentially recognises only three generations; his own, his father's and his grand father's, and that the terms of address fully indicate the merging of grandfather's generation with that of the Ego.

Turning to Ego's Mother's lineage, we find that one addresses one's mother's brother, elder or younger, by the term *Mama*. Indeed, all male members having the standing of brothers to one's mother would be called *Mama* and the *Mama* in turn would address the Ego as *Mamu*. Mother's father is addressed as *Nana* or *Baba* and he may also in turn address Ego as *Nana* or *Baba*. Any member of further ascending generations would be addressed by the same term, that is, *Nana* or *Baba* and would reciprocate by these terms. The mother's sisters are addressed by the term *Mausi* and are regarded as mothers though the usage has it that Ego's father cannot marry Ego's mother's elder sister. The wive's maternal uncles, on the other hand, are addressed as *Fua* or *Mami* and they in turn address Ego as *Damad* (or affectionately *bacha* meaning child).

One does not address his wife, among the Bharias, by name. She is addressed "mother of so and so" (technonymy) but until such time she has a child her attention may be drawn by the husband by speaking loudly, or if she is inside the house by simply saying what one has to say. But there is no term of address by which a Bharia may call his wife. Wife's father is addressed by the term *Mamu.* Wife's father's father would be addressed by the term *Baba* and he would, in turn, address Ego by the term *Nati* or *Bhaiya.*

There are no terms of address for mother's brother's daughters and fathers's sister's daughters. The Bharias say that when Ego and they are of the same age they call each other *Goin* which literally means partners in game or play. But should Ego marry one of the sisters the younger sisters would address him by the term *Jeeja* and elder sisters would call him *Damad.* The elder and younger brothers of Ego's wife, on the other hand, would address him as *Samdhi* because Ego's son may claim the hand of his father's sister's daughter. The husbands of girls related as sisters address each other by the term *Bhai* and are referred to as *Sadhu.*

It may be mentioned here that the terms of kinship appear to have been derived from the Bundelkhandi dialect. Even though Patalkot does not form part of Bundelkhand, it is not very far from there; the Bundelkhandi influence on the kinship terminology is unmistakable. The kinship terms have been passed down from generations and, needless to mention, they have remained unchanged to the day. There is no evidence to suggest that at any stage of their existence the Bharias have taken to these terms in place of another set of their own, because even a trace of any ancient set of terms does not exist among them. The kinship system, it may be added, is more stable than the social fabric of the society.

Kinship and its functions

One of the fundamental functions of kinship is to regulate marriage, and among the Bharias the kinship usage makes it obligatory on certain relatives to provide their daughters as wives to specific relatives. We find that cross-cousin marriages, both with paternal aunt's daughter (FaSis Dau) and maternal uncle's daughter (MoBrDau), are put by the Bharias in the category of "preferential mates." The following diagram would show the two types of cross-cousin marriages.

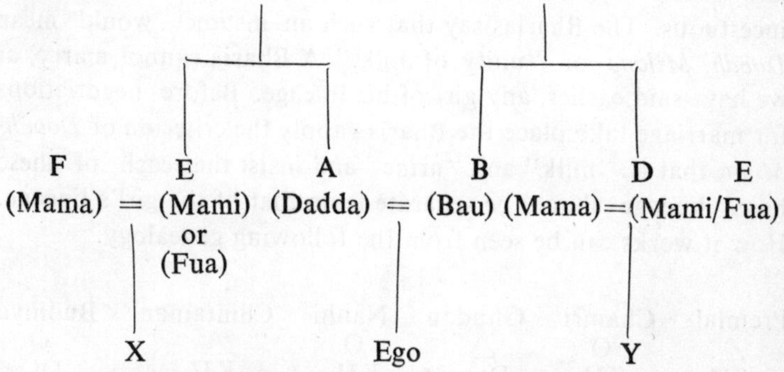

Here, it may be seen that X and Y are Ego's potential mates. According to Bharia custom if a person addresses another by as *Mama* then the latter's daughter is regarded as a potential mate for him. The fact that mother's brother, and father's sister's husband are addressed by the same term *Mama*, which one uses for his wife's father, shows that the two of them stand as potential fathers-in-law to Ego and their daughters are potential spouses of the latter. Thus it will be seen that the marriage has influenced the Bharias' kinship terms. It also shows the interlocking of relationship in the two families which, generation after generation, may be renewed and reinforced by such marriages. The Bharias say that marriages are arranged only with *Mama's* daughters. If the mother's brother or father's sister has no daughters, the choice may be made from among the daughters of classificatory relatives addressed as *Mama*.

A Bharia can marry one or more younger sisters of his wife, because wife's sisters are classed as potential wives. But he cannot marry the elder sister of his wife with whom he must "keep respectable distances." She is regarded as *Jad Sas*, a relative placed in the same category, so to say, as *Sas* or mother-in-law, and yet different. But if a woman standing in such relationship to Ego marries his elder brother, the element of "respectable distance" is ignored and she may be addressed as *Bhabhi*.

A Bharia cannot marry any of his mother's sisters because mother's sisters are regarded as mothers, though one or two of them may be of the same age as Ego. The children of mother's sisters are regarded as falling within the category of "brothers and sisters" and a union between the two would be regarded incestuous. The Bharias say that such an instance would mean *Doodh Milana* or "unity of milk." A Bharia cannot marry, as we have said earlier, any girl of his lineage. Before negotiations for marriage take place the Bharias apply the criterion of *Doodh-Moot*, that is, "milk" and "urine" and insist that each of these boys' lineage should be separate from that of the girl's lineage. How it works can be seen from the following genealogy:

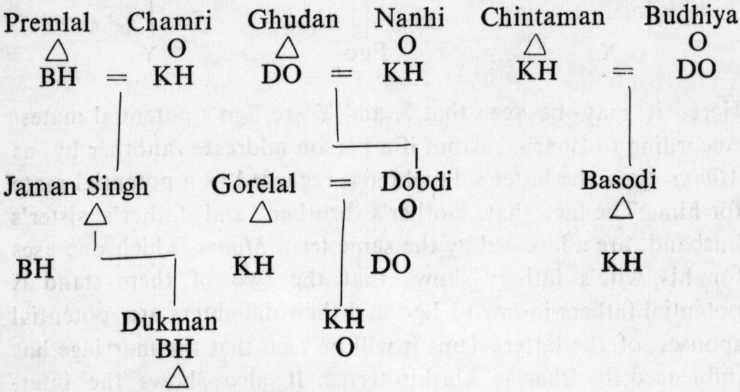

BH = Bhardiya Clan
DO = Dandioliya Clan
KH = Khamariya Clan

In the above genealogy, Chamri and Nanhi, are shown as real sisters, one married to Premlal (BH) and the other to Ghudan (DO). Now Dobdi who is the daughter of Nanhi and Ghudan could not have been taken in marriage by Jaman Singh, the son of Chamri and Premlal. This is because Jaman and Dobdi are interlinked to each other through mothers who are sisters and so have "unity of milk". But in the descending generation, Jaman Singh's son Dukman can marry the daughter of Dobdi and Gorelal, because in this generation the "unity of milk" is lost. On the other hand, Chintaman's son Basodi, to whom Dobdi is only father's sister's daughter, could have taken her in marriage. Indeed she would have been a potential mate for him, but such a marriage did not take place because Basodi is young and Dobdi now the mother of a child. Within the lineage a man cannot marry because such a union would mean incest caused by, as the Bharias, say "unity of urine". The Bharias say that before negotiations for marriage can take place they "strain" the "milk" and the "urine" in the above manner.

The kinship system of the Bharias has shown great persistence through the passage of time and passing of generations. Its essential features exhibited in classificatory terminology, cross-cousin marriage and "avoidance" between specific relatives have been maintained, so far. The internal structure of relations involved has, of course, undergone change. Thus the parents and fathers and mothers-in-law are no longer given the same kind of respect as they received two generations ago or earlier. Similarly, the members of a particular segment of the patrilineage do not exhibit the same solidarity in certain social situations today as in the times of their grandfathers.

Clan organisation

The Bharia term *got*, which appears to be a variation of the Sanskrit word *gotra*, denotes clan. As indicated earlier the Bharia clans are patrilineal and the reckoning of descent as well as inheritance are in the paternal line. The Bharias are not good at remembering their genealogies beyond the grandfather's generation, and even in this, second ascending generation, the links in the genealogical trees are remembered only by the old persons and more often in respect of males only. This means that if one wishes to demonstrate the genealogical connection amongst all the members of a particular clan, he cannot establish an interlinked lineage structure because beyond the second or third ascending generation the names of ancestors linking one lineage to another lineage within the clan are forgotten. Nevertheless, all the members of clan have a feeling of belonging to a particular clan.

The Bharias say that originally in their tribe there were only twelve-and-a-half *gots*. Twelve clans were those of the Bharias and the half-a-clan was that of the *Bhats* or traditional singers whose job was to recite the names of Bharia ancestors and sing their praise. The *Bhats* also sing in praise of Gonds. Though it is not clear as to why half-a-clan of *Bhats* should be said to be included among the Bharia *gots*, it is possible that during old times, a lineage of *Bhats* might have settled in Patalkot, a lineage which formed part of some important clan of the *Bhats*. But at present there are no families of *Bhats* anywhere in Patalkot or in its vicinity, nor is there any evidence to suggest that there were any *Bhats* two generations ago.

The Bharias say that formerly when a Bharia died, the *Bhat* associated with the family of the deceased received a brass plate, an axe, a cow and the deceased's clothes. The customary payment was made for *mailchun* or "removing dirt". It was only after the *Bhat* had done the purificatory rite that the family became "ritually pure". This being one of the important functions of the *Bhat* in the old days, it can be inferred that the Bharias did not consider them as being low in the social strata. It seems that to keep them satisfied they might have regarded them as though they were half-Bharia or half of a Bharia clan.

Even if originally there were 12 clans of the Bharias, this is certainly not the case today. The Bharias while speaking of their tribe include as many as 19 clans in the list. Surely not all clans are found in the Patalkot valley. The significant point of including the entire list of Bharia clans here is that it is largely within the universe of these clans that the Bharias of Patalkot recognise and place their own clans. Each clan bears a name which has a reference to some episode with the original ancestor, though his name is forgotten. The 19 clans identified by the Bharias of Patalkot and the legends of their origin are given in Table 6.

Though 19 clans are enumerated by the informants, only eight of them could be identified by the genealogical survey of four villages in the valley. The distribution of clans in the four villages is given in Table 7.

TABLE 6: The 19 clans with legends of their origin

Name of the Clan	Legend of origin
Bharadhiya	They came from a place called Bhardagarh and called themselves Bharadhiya.
Khamariya	Khamariya were named after the *Khamer* tree. Khamaria clansmen do not eat fruits of Khamer tree.
Panchaliya	Pachaliya or Khud-Pachaliya means a ditch for throwing rubbish. They originated from such a ditch.
Bagothiya	He hid himself near the shadow of *Bagh* or tiger, hence his descendants were called by this name.
Angariya	*Angar* means fire, and the ancestors of this clan sat near a fire burning in the field. Hence they were called Angariya.
Bijaliya	*Bijili* is lightning. He saw lightning and fell down. Others saw him and called him Bijaliya.
Dandioliya	*Dandi* means a man's beard. Since he tried to hide himself in the beard, his descendants were called by this name. But some Bharias say that *dandi* is a stick and members of this clan do not fix a stick to plough or *bakkhar*.
Chalathiya	When others sat down to take rest, he continued walking and was, therefore, called *Chalathiya* which means one who walks much.
Routhi a	*Routhiya* is one who keeps weeping. While others talked and laughed he kept weeping. So he and his descendants were called *Routhiya*.
Thakariya	While walking, footfalls of some animals make the sound *thak thak*. He caught a leg of the animal when the sound stopped. He was therefore called *Thakariya*.
Kanchiholiya	*Kanch* is a part of *dhoti* which a man passes in between his legs and tucks to his waist at the back. It is said that one of the ancestors while walking his son caught his *kanch*, and therefore he was called *Kanchiholiya*.

Table 6 (contd.)

Nahaliya	He way very fond of bathing. *Nahaliya* means "one who is fond of taking bath" hence his descendants were called *Nahaliya*.
Mahaniya	He "agreed" to do something for another man who stopped him. He agreed and was called *Mahaniya*.
Gwaliya	In ancient time, there was a fort at a place called Gwaliagarh*. The ancestor of *Gwalia* clansmen was fond of climbing to the Gwalia hill and was, therefore, called *Gwalia*.
Kudamiya	*Kudamiya* is one who speaks slowly to himself. While taking rest he used to speak to himself in this manner.
Bagdariya	*Bagda* means a fly. One of the ancestors used to play with and kill flies, so that his children were called *Bagdariya*.
Kundaliya	Near him a snake sat coild or in *Kundali*, so he was called *Kundaliya*.
Bilai Koliya	He touched the tail of a cat (*Bilai*) and was called *Bilai Koliya*.
Amodiya	Not known.

*This appears to be Deogarh, the seat of "Gwali" kings who were killed by Jatbasa the first.

TABLE 7: **Distribution of the eight identified clans in four villages**

Name of the clan	No. of households in each village			
	Rated	Kaream	Dodiparna	Harra-kachhar
Bharadhiya	2	—	1	—
Dandioliya	2	4	1	5
Angariya	3	—	2	—
Khamariya	8	1	1	1
Bagdariya	1	—	—	—
Pachaliya	1	—	1	—
Amodiya	—	5	—	—
Chalathiya	—	—	1	—
Total	17	10	7	6

Though these figures relate to only four Bharia villages, it is apparent that the tendency of the members of a lineage of a particular clan is to live together. Khamariyas, for example, are concentrated in Rated, Dandioliyas in Harrakachhar and Kaream and Amodiyas in Kaream. The presence of nearly half of the Bharia clans (in spite of uneven population of each) provides them the opportunity of selecting spouses within the same village or villages within the Patalkot valley though, as will be seen later, Bharias frequently marry outside Patalkot. The possibility of a Bharia clan claiming a territorial jurisdiction in the past cannot be ruled out, but it cannot be substantiated.

Two of the Bharia clans of Patalkot have fraternal relationship with two other Bharia clans, by extension of the *Bhaiband relationship*, the Kundaliya clansmen living in Dudhaniya and Batkidhana villages near Bijori—some 16 kilometres away. They say that this relationship is being maintained by them since the times of *aja-paraja* or great grandfathers, which to them means more than five generations. Similarly Bharadhiya clansmen regard Bagdariya clansmen as their *bhaiband*. These are, however, the only two pairs of clans in Patalkot valley which show fraternal relationship and follow the rule of exogamy as a unit. A Khamariya marrying a Kundaliya and vice versa, or a Bharadhiya marrying a Bagdariya would amount to an incest today in the same way as it could be two generations ago.

Cleavage of clans

Within a few clans, the lineages, though their vertical depth can scarcely be measured,have specific names and these names have originated due to a particular social situation occurring at some period beyond three to four generations. The cleavage in Pachaliya and Bharadhiya clans are as follows: Pachaliyas are divided into (i) Pachaliya; (ii) Khud Panchaliya; and (iii) Banda Pachaliya. Pachaliyas were indeed one clan but the members of a certain lineage became so few that parents kept a tuft of hair on the head of their child and promised to deities that if he survived they would shave off the tuft seating him on the heap of rubbish. Luckily the child survived and they fulfilled their promises and were called *Khud* (meaning a ditch) *Pachaliya*. Banda Pachaliya were so called because during the marriage they killed a pig for a feast, *banda* meaning a pig. Indeed Banda Pachaliya are the only lineage who live in Patalkot in Dodipara and Rated villages. Two generations ago it was customary for a Banda Pachaliya to kill a pig half of which was given to the bride's party and the other half to the relatives of the groom. The custom, however, has undergone a change under outside influence. The sacrificial pig was replaced by a goat, a far humbler animal. In the recent years it has further been simplified: now a big lump of jaggery is divided into two pieces in place of a goat. The Bharadhiya clan is likewise divided into Khiya Bharadhiya and Dhangur-Bharadhiya. Those who belong to Khiya lineage do not eat the flesh of *Khiya* bird (babbler) and do not touch it. This custom is still observed by the Khiya-Bharadhiya of Patalkot who live in Rated. The Dhangur Bharadhiya who are said to live in Sarkadhana village outside Patalkot valley formerly wore a piece of cloth around the waist.

Clan and totem

The Bharia clans are totemic in nature. We have mentioned above that Khiya Bharadhiya do not eat or touch Khiya bird. The Khamariya clansmen do not eat fruits of *Khamer* tree nor do they touch a kind of gum. If a Khamariya man touches it, the persisting custom is that he must take a bath of oil and water. Unless the purificatory rite is performed none would permit him to enter his house for the fear that he would be struck with misery. Bagothiya and Bagdariya should never kill a tiger because it is their totem animal. We may mention here that the taboos such as these have only symbolic importance because the animals and birds such as *Khiya* or a tiger, or a small fruit such as *Khamer*, are not at all important from the point of view of food supply. It merely remains for a Bharia to tell you that he wouldn't kill a tiger because some ancestor was saved by him, or would not kill *Khiya* because the bird helped him in some great difficulty.

Functions of clan

As for the functions of a Bharia clan it is noticeable that the clans are not corporate groups which can be said to act as a unit on any specific occasion. The clans are dispersed not only within the valley but also outside it, and the members living 16 to 20 kilometres away cannot be expected to act as corporate groups. The most essential function of the clan is exogamy which follows from the belief of common descent, a common name and common taboos. A funeral of a patrikin would not involve the attendance of all the clan members. Much would depend upon the distance at which the other segments of the clan of the deceased live. But here, it is the patrikin with closer ties who would come; those who are "distant" may not oblige unless they have personal reasons to do so. The effective area of cooperation is limited and the limit seems to be set partly by distance and partly by the patrikin themselves who consider themselves "close" or "near".

Marriage

Clan exogamy and tribe endogamy are the accepted norms of the Bharia society. It is a rarity to see a Bharia marrying outside his tribe. Clan exogamy is strictly adhered to as anyone flouting this rule does an incestuous act. Regarding village (territorial) exogamy or endogamy, there is no hard and fast rule. One may marry either within his village or outside, provided the spouse does not belong to the "avoidance" group. There are instances of Bharia men and women marrying even from outside the Patalkot valley, although such instances are not many.

A Bharia man may marry more than once, if his economic resources permit. But many young Bharias find it difficult, as they say, to get married even once. This situation is supported by the statistics that there are more males in proportion to females. In the Patalkot valley the Bharias number 360 males as against 340 females, that is to say, there are 944 females for every 1,000 males. And if we take the ratio of Bharia males and females or Bharia-Bhumia as they have returned themselves in the Census of 1971 (tribewise population of 1981 not yet available), we find that the ratio of Bharia females to males for the entire district of Chhindwara (935) is very near to that for Patalkot.

In such a society polygyny is only incidental. In the genealogical sample of 24 families it was found that there were only two persons in Rated—Jeevan Bharia and Bhondal Bharia—each of whom has two wives. A Bharia with more than two wives is a rarity. A Bharia may have another wife after the death or divorce of the first one. It may also be noted that a Bharia girl can be married only once in her lifetime; if she runs away from her first husband, she may go to live with another man under the *Kaarta* custom, but she cannot be "married" to him.

Bharias marry, normally, when they attain majority or in their own words, "when they are capable of standing on their own feet". A boy marries "when he wore turban and became able to shoulder the domestic and agricultural responsibilities". The girls, on the other hand, are given away in marriage only after puberty.

The genealogical studies show that adult marriage had been the rule even in the past. While parents gave due importance to the relative ages of the boy and the girl, considerations of establishing new, or reinforcing the old ties with the particular family often carried greater weight than the consideration of age. 'My wife is almost three years older then me in age"; said Jangal Singh, "but her father prevailed upon my father when I was young. I was shy to protest and simply kept quiet. I had to obey my parents, and we were married". Times have changed since. The boys and girls have now considerable freedom in saying "yes" or "no" to a marriage proposal, and full weight is given to their opinion. "It is no use going against the wishes of a girl", said Chamru Bharia of Daudipara, "because if she does not like her husband, she would run away to another man. If a boy does not like his wife, there would be quarrels and the girl would have to leave him."

A Bharia's marriage involves payment of bride-price—*kodon kutki*, liquor and cloth to the bride's father. It is actually this payment which transfers the right of the father over the girl to her husband. The rights so transferred include sexual rights, rights over a woman's procreative powers, rights over domestic services, rights over her economic services and right of living together. On the other hand, the husband's obligations are to provide the wife with shelter and food, clothes and ornaments according to his ability, treat her well, and to observe fidelity. Indeed, observance of fidelity to each other is reckoned to be an important factor for stability of the family. If either is unfaithful, the marriage may break; and it is always the girl who runs away to her parents or to her new companion. In either case the matter is eventually brought before the council of elders for a solution.

A marriage among the Bharias may be brought about by one of the following four methods: The first method is by negotiations between the two families. The second is marriage by service, in which case the boy may work at the prospective father-in-law's house as a *lamjhana*. In a *lamjhana* marriage the boy's father is not required to incur any expenditure save something on the *sagai* or betrothal. The third method is elopement in which case the spouses simply run away. If a boy and a girl are in love with each other they usually run away to a relative's place only to be discovered by the parents later on. The marriage ceremoney, in this case, is usually conducted in the same manner as for marrige by negotiations though some of the important rites are waived. It is, however, fundamentally important that the boy and the girl should not stand in a prohibited kin relationship. Yet another kind of marriage occurs when a girl forcibly enters the house of the husband straightaway. This is called *Ghusri* or marriage by intrusion. In such cases no marriage rites are performed. The *Panchas* (elders) are given a feast called *pat-roti*. Once the feast is over they are socially recognised as man and wife. The most prevalent among the abovementioned modes of acquiring the mate is by negotiation or marriage by service. The other two methods are very seldom resorted to and, in fact, none was reported in the field. Since the institution of *lamjhana* (marriage by service) is of great importance to the Bharias, it is discussed below in some detail before considering the arranged marriage.

The lamsana or lamjhana marriage

The institution of *lamsana* or *lamjhana*, under which a boy is required to serve in the house of his prospective father-in-law for a period ranging from three to four years before he marries the girl has existed among the Bharias since time immemorial. The institution is also known to be existing among the neighbouring Gonds[1] and is one of the important ways in which a young man is enabled to secure a wife for himself. It has already been indicated that the Bharias are on the whole poor and many of them find it often difficult to get their sons married with the limited resources at their command. One of the accepted practices, therefore, is to compensate the bride's father by way of rendering personal labour, who then agrees to forgo the bride-price that he would ask for his daughter otherwise.

There are, however, certain important considerations to be taken into account before a young Bharia can enter the *lamjhana* service. First, and of paramount importance, is that the prospective *lamjhana* should be an accepted member of the community. Since the institution implies "marriage by service" a non-Bharia (a Gond, for instance) cannot be accepted as a *lamjhana*. The other considerations, equally important, are those that apply to marriage among the Bharias in general. Thus a *lamjhana* should not stand in relationship to the girl that would be within the prohibited degree of marriage. This implies that he should belong to a clan other than that of his prospective bride.

A boy, when he enters the service of the prospective father-in-law, is usually 12 or 13 years old, so that when he ends his tenure of service, he is mature enough to marry the girl. The Bharias say that a grown-up man would neither like to come to work as *lamjhana* nor would be suitable for a young girl. Any great disparity in age is only well known to lead to matrimonial discord and breaking of the families. A very young boy is also not likely to be accepted as a *lamjanna* because he would not be able to work to the satisfaction of the family. Another essential point is that the boy should be able to stay and work in the father-in-law's house for full three years and should not ordinarily give a chance to the family members for annoyance.

The lamjhana contract

The Bharias say that the *lamjhana* agreement cannot be a quiet affair made between two persons and without the knowledge of others. The village elders have to meet in the boy's or an elder's house to listen to both the parties. The boy's father then makes a formal proposal to the girl's father, to the effect that he would like to keep his son as *lamjhana*. Usually the girl's father agrees to the proposal, having made up his mind already, or else there could be no necessity for a meeting of the *Panchas*. The tribal elders are entertained by the boy's father with some food and drinks. The occasion then becomes an evidence of the agreement reached. The manner in which the *lamjhana* agreement is reached has so far not undergone any change.

The time when the prospective father-in-law invites the *lamjhana* to work in his house is usually the month of *Jeth* corresponding to June of the Gregorian calendar. This is the time when there is considerable work relating to agriculture. A *lamjhana* is expected to begin the work at the beginning of the month in the fields and also assist the members of the family in the domestic chores.

A boy who comes to work as a *lamjhana* from another house in the same village, or even a village not too distant, usually finds the new home almost as comfortable as his own. The girl's parents and even the girl call him by the term *lamjhana*. The word is not derogatory and does not mean a paid servant. A *lamjhana* from the day he comes to the girl's house, is provided with food which is no different from the food shared by other members of the family. He is given space to sleep in the house and taken care of during illness. He is not expected to do more work than a boy of his age normally does. He may visit his parental home at times, but is not expected to remain there for many days. Nor does the *lamjhana* work for his parents; that must be left to his other brothers. Custom demands that the *lamjhana's* father accept no work from him, and should he be called upon to do some job, it would be with the permission of his prospective father-in-law. The latter can also claim the earnings of the *lamjhana* because "any work my *lamjhana* does", said Chintaman Bharia, "is my family matter and I can claim his earnings."

The *lamjhana* is expected to give due respect to the girl's parents and this implies that he should obey them as he would obey his parents. As a rule no quarrels are expected between the *lamjhana* and the parents of the girl. Should an occasion arise the *lamjhana* must submit, he is not expected to retort. During his tenure of service a *lamjhana* must behave well, as a member of the family. Formerly a *lamjhana* was not even expected to smoke *chilam* (earthen pipe) in the presence of his father-in-law. The custom has since undergone change and a *lamjhana* may refrain from it at the beginning but may smoke in the presence of his father-in-law in due course.

During the "service" period of *lamjhana* he is not customarily permitted to cultivate intimacy with the girl. No physical relationship can be established until after the girl has been married to him. The Bharias say that though the *lamjhana* lives in the same house as the girl, he would ordinarily avoid talking to her. Similarly the girl also would avoid him. But they opined that "none could stand guard for night and day", if they ventured to have physical relations that could only be at their peril, for if discovered they would be put to shame. The two *lamjhana* working in Rated village said that they considered it shameful and never thought of sexual game with the girls whom they would marry in due course, anyway. Moreover, if a girl became pregnant it would not only be shameful, they added, but also involve the boy's parents into trouble. Customarily the tribal Panchayat imposes a fine on the boy's father as well as on the girl's father for the misdeed of their children. Thus, fear of pregnancy, fear of shame and the fine by the *Panchas* keep the *lamjhana* on the proper path. The Bharias could not recollect a single instance of a girl becoming pregnant from a *lamjhana*.

Completion of service

Normally, as already indicated, a *lamjhana's* service period extends to only three years and before the beginning of the fourth year he is expected to return to his paternal home. It is characteristic of the *lamjhana* institution that once the obligation of service is over, the girl's father should prepare for her marriage with the *lamjhana*. The boy's father is customarily absolved from the payment of bride-price and actually establishes a claim upon the girl's father who alone must incur all expenditure on the marriage ceremony. In many cases the girl's father who is economically well off may prepare for the marriage within a few months. But there are instances in which the actual marriage may be deferred even by a year. When this happens the girl's father requests the boy's father before the Panchayat that the *lamjhana* should be allowed to continue to live in his house for one more year. To give an example, Premlal Bharia's son who worked in the house of Chintaman as a *lamjhana* for three years could not be married soon after the obligatory period of service since Chintaman could not collect sufficient grains for the feast and the payment during marriage. He, therefore, made a request to Premlal that the marriage be postponed. Premlal agreed before the *Panchas* that the *lamjhana* should continue to live in Chintaman's house until the following year. Since Chintaman also had a son he wished to celebrate the marriage of his son as well as his daughter at the same time to avoid expenditure on feeding the *Panchas* and the relatives, at two different occasions.

It is obligatory on the part of the girl's father to give his daughter in marriage to the *lamjhana*, but there are instances when a girl may run away with another man before her marriage with the *lamjhana*. This, for instance, happened in the case of Bajara son of Ghudan who worked as a *lamjhana* for securing the hand of Oli, the daughter of Bhondal Bharia. Before Bajara was able to complete three years' service in the house of Bhondal, Oli ran away with a young man called Santlal of Sootiya village of the erstwhile Pagara *Jagir*. Bhondal had no alternative but to give Bajara a bullock for the service he had rendered. The custom of giving a bullock in such cases has persisted. The bullock is said to be given for *Dartodana* or "ending the dispute." Now a sum of Rs 200/ can also be given in lieu of and will be acceptable to the *lamjhana's* father. While the *lamjhana* could have no complaint against Bhondal he would continue to nurse a grudge against Santlal. According to Bharia custom Santlal is required not only to make a settlement with Bhondal but also to provide two bullocks or at least Rs 200/ to Bajara, in addition to a feast to the *Panchas* who would eventually bring about the settlement of the dispute.

Arranged marriage

Procedure and rites: A Bharia's difficulty in securing a suitable girl for his son is, broadly speaking, created by two factors: his economic poverty and the custom of cross-cousin marriage. The latter custom makes it obligatory on a Bharia to restrict his choice to the girls who are his cross-cousins.

Once the boy's parents choose the girl, the first step is to visit the girl's house known as *modi-mangna* (ask for the girl) with five *chappatis* (cakes) of maize and a bottle of liquor, distilled locally or purchased from the local liquor shop. On reaching the house the boy's father exchanges greetings with the girl's father by saying *Ram Ram.* The Bharias call this *Ram Bhalai.* Soon after this he is offered water to wash his face, feet and hands. This done, they sit down and the purpose of the visit (often already known) is disclosed. The boy's father offers the girl's father the five maize *chappatis* and the bottle of liquor. If the girl's father accepts these presents, it implies that he is prepared to give his daughter in marriage. The girl's parents eat the *chappatis*, drink liquor and, in return, offer food to them. Village elders assemble and discuss the main issues related to marriage before the boy's parents return.

The second step is the betrothal or *sagai.* This is an important occasion. The rite, briefly described below, takes place at the girl's house. Information is sent in advance to all the relatives. Those who are related to the girl—maternal and paternal kins—assemble at the girl's house; and those related to the boy gather at the boy's house. A case history of a *Sagai* rite observed in Dodipara village provides sufficient insight.

The groom's father Bhangra of Amodiya clan, who lives in Kaream, was a poor Bharia. He sent his son to work in the house of Najaru Bharia of Dodipara village. Najaru belonged to the Angariya clan. He kept the boy as a servant on the understanding that should he continue working in his house

1. Distant view of a village

2. A typical Bharia

3. A young Bharia girl

4. A Bharia house

5. 'Usari' of a Bharia house

6. The 'tonge' for keeping maize corns

. At the market

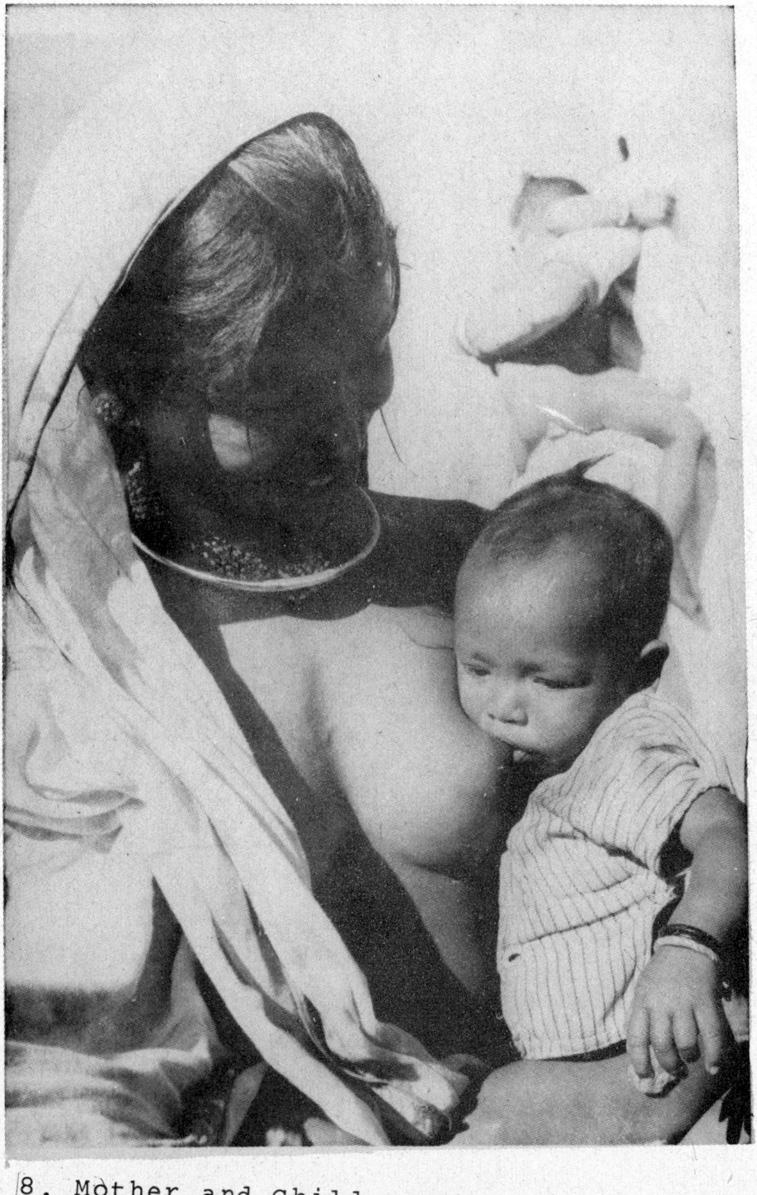

8. Mother and Child

9. A typical Bharia house

for three years, he would arrange and incur all the expenditure on his marriage It was, therefore, Najaru who had arranged for the boy's betrothal with Ramwati, the eldest daughter of Jugru Bharia of *Dandioliya* clan living in the same village.

The boy's relatives, men and women, living in Kaream, Dodipara, Rated, Chintipur and Harra-Kachhar villages feasted in Najaru's house. Whatever food the women could not eat they wrapped up in leaves and carried home. The male members, soon after the feast, formed into a procession. They carried *kotoki* (a kind of grain), jaggery, salt and liquor with them. Each of them customarily carried a stick. Soon they reached the girl's house, where men were ready to receive them and the women had gathered to sing songs. The bride's brother was ready with water, and a woman, related to the bride, poured water and washed the feet of each guest. This done, they entered the single-roomed house of Jugru and sat inside. The women sitting in the verandah sang songs appropriate to the occasion.

After a while the *kotoki* was put before the bride's relatives. One of them measured it with a metal *paili* or *pai* (a measure) and finding it 20 measures—to the satisfaction of everyone—sent it to be cooked. Premlal Bhumka of Rated, a maternal uncle of the bride, acted as the priest, lit a lamp, poured some liquor on the floor and offered a few *kharaks* (dried dates) to the ancestors of the lineage. Holding the lamp in his right hand he moved it to and fro thrice and the *Arati* (evils) of the departed was removed. He prayed to the ancestors to witness the *sagai* and bless the two families with a strong lasting relationship. The turn now came for the *samandhi bhet* or "hugging" of the boy's and girl's parents. The boy's father offered liquor to the bride's father who reciprocated and said, "today I make a promise, in front of all, that I am giving my daughter to Bangra, Amoriya's son". After a drink, sitting as they were in front of each other, they stretched hands and embraced each other thrice. The mother of the boy and the mother of the girl met neck-to-neck in the same manner. The women continued singing; the rite was over. What everyone expected now was the feast. Liquor was served to men and women in leaf-cups who drank liberally after offering libation to the ancestors.

At about 3.30 p.m. the men and women were requested to sit in two rows. The bride's people served them cooked *kotoki* and lentils. All of them ate the food served on leaf plates except an ironsmith who, though living in the village, would not eat the Bharia's cooked food. Before the relatives left they received presents of jaggery to carry home. But many relatives stayed back for the night to drink and make merry.

The Bharias consider the *Sagai* rite (also called *Deej ka Baithak*) of great importance. It is a formal expression of the agreement arrived at between two families to create a lasting relationship by offering subsequently a girl from her body of kin to anolher kin-group. The occasion is witnessed by the living and is believed to be watched by the departed; the promise made by the girl's parents is considered absolutely firm "like a rock", as Halku Bharia puts it.

The third step is the performance of final rites. Once these rites are over, the Bharia boy and the girl are said to have become man and wife. Two generations ago, the parents of the groom would visit the bride's house with their relatives carrying one *khandi* of *kotoki*, three to five seers of jaggery, salt and liquor. The bride's father accepted the articles as bride price and indicated the day on which he would bring the girl to the boy's house. The *bhanware* (going round the carved pillar), which is the most important marriage rite, was performed at the boy's house. The custom has, however, undergone change during the past two generations and the *bhanware* is now performed at the girl's house.

A few days earlier to her marriage, the bride along with her two or three friends visits the houses of her paternal relatives. Her friends apart, her sister's husband, known as *sawasia* accompanies for the duration of the marriage rites. The bride is required to cover her face and cry loudly, "O Kaka why you are expelling me from the house where I have been so happy." "O Kaki why you want me to leave my parental home." The *sawasia* shows the way to the bride and her friends while the other related women follow her. On reaching a relative's house one of the inmates washes the feet of the guests, and requests the party to sit down. The bride continues crying intermittently.

The women relatives sit down near her and console her. After this, the relatives offer them food. The bride then gives a turmeric root and some rice to the eldest female relative and requests, through her, all the inmates of the house to come to her marriage. The groom, on the other hand, extends invitation to his relatives. He also offers them a piece of turmeric and some rice. These customs have persisted among the Bharias and so far there is no noticeable change in them.

On the day of marriage the groom and his relatives arrive at the girl's house. In the morning of that day turmeric powder is smeared on the boy and the girl by their sisters. This is done seven times, starting from feet to the face and then seven times from the face to the feet. The drummers arrive and beat the drums at the bride's house. The important rite is the *bhanware* and it is performed under a *mandwa* or small pandal. The Bharias make a pandal with wooden posts and thatch it with twigs and leaves. They fasten to the pandal festoons of mango leaves. In the middle of this pandal a pillar, about three feet high and made of a branch of *hardu* tree, is fixed in the ground. The pillar, usually carved with the traditional Bharia designs, is called *munda*.

The bride, dressed and wearing ornaments, is attended to by three women who are called *lagni*. They are usually relatives who are customarily given presents of cloth for their services. Before the marriage takes place they sing the traditional songs. They bring the girl near the carved post and ask her to go round it. The girl is expected to refuse to do so and weep. This behaviour of the girl is resisted by the boy who eventually catches her by hand and makes her go round the carved post seven times. After the *bhanware* the boy and the girl sit down and the boy, according to custom, presses her leg with his knee and thigh. This is to assert his authority and the claim over the girl; after this the marriage is supposed to be over.

After *bhanware* a feast is given by the boy's father. On reaching the doors of the boy's house, the boy's younger brother referred to as *dewar* throws a small stick towards her, standing in front of the door. This he does thrice and the bride has to pick it up and touch it to her forehead. After this rite she enters the house. After a day or two the bride and bridegroom are expected to go to the river to take a purificatory bath. The boys and the girls of the village usually follow them and tease them. While taking bath the woman is expected to rub the back of her husband, thus displaying her faith in serving him. After the bath is over the party returns home.

On the same day, the boy's parents invite the members of the village, clansmen and relatives and serve them food and liquor. This is called *sukh-mandee.* After this feast the husband and wife may sleep together.

Jangal Singh said: "This used to be so in our days. We could not think of sleeping with the wife until all relatives went away. But nowadays boys and girls do not care. Formerly a newly wed boy never talked to his father-in-law and mother-in-law; nowadays some of them openly quarrel on small matters." So, according to him, the authority of the "old" is being eroded and respect for the old is "declining".

Secondary unions

The Bharia society does not permit remarriage of a woman who has lost her husband. She may, however, be "kept" by one of the younger brothers of the deceased, married or unmarried. This is called *Bithalna.* Thus the society specifically provides for junior levirate. An elder brother of the deceased cannot marry his deceased younger brother's wife. This would be an infringement of the custom. He is referred to as *Jeth* by the woman, and the Bharias say that he is regarded as *Bhagwan.* A *Jeth* is held in the same esteem as the father-in-law. Nevertheless a case of an elder brother taking his younger brother's wife occurred more than 20 years ago.

Jeevan Bharia's elder brother had a wife whom he could not make happy. The result was that after some months of her marriage she ran away to her parental home. The matter came before the village elders and they decided that the girl's father should pay two bullocks as compensation to Jeevan's brother. The bullocks were given as decided and so the case was amicably settled. Jeevan's brother, however, soon got entangled with

Jeevan's first wife and one day he eloped with her. Jeevan complained to the village elders who decided that he should be excommunicated. He now lives in a distant village called Gotikhera. Bharias say that as long as he is alive no Bharia would accept water from him. His brother Jeevan would not permit him to approach the interior of the house near the *Deokholi* (temple), since that would displease the deities.

The Bharias also have a custom which provides for secondary union of a widow with a person other than the younger brother of the deceased. A woman who runs away to her parental home and thus gets "separated" or one who is divorced may settle with another Bharia, if he does not fall within the category of "prohibited" relatives. Such provisions, which were prevalent generations ago, continue to persist and their persistence allows widowers to have a wife and a family. No elaborate rites are performed in this type of union. The *Panchas* of the widower's village approach the *Panchas* of the widow's village. After an agreement is reached, the widower is required to offer them Rs 5 worth of jaggery and liquor. He must also give Rs. 1.25 to the *Kotwar* (village watchman) and Rs. 1.25 to *Mukaddam* (village head), after which the woman is sent to live with the widower. Before the woman enters the new house the couple must sprinkle water mixed with turmeric powder on each other. The couple are then required to give a small feast to the village elders. Such unions are said to be *Kaarta* or "keeping", and are reckoned of small significance by the Bharias. The couple, however, obtain status as husband and wife and their children have the same status as those whose parents married with *bhanware* rite. If a woman brings a child from her previous husband to her new husband's house, the child is reared for some years and then given to his father's family. The father is customarily required to compensate the guardian by paying Rs 50 or a small cow.

REFERENCE

1. Kurup, A. M., "Bride Price Among the Gonds," *Bulletin* of the Tribal Research Institute, Vol. IV, No. 1, 1964. Chhindwara, Madhya Pradesh.

5

RELIGIOUS LIFE

THE MAIN features of the Bharias' religious system are: universal belief in a Supreme Being and a number of smaller gods or deities, prescribed procedures and rituals for their propitiation, the priesthood and procedures for curing the sick, magical beliefs, and finally belief in the soul and life after death. These features in the context of the Bharia religion are essentially "tribal", but it may be mentioned at the outset that Hindu religious beliefs and practices have also made considerable impact on the Bharias. Such impact is not recent; the knowledge and acceptance of Hindu gods, their propitiation with coconut and dried dates and the celebration of such Hindu festivals as Holi, Diwali and Dussehra clearly appear to have been accepted quite early. The present-day Bharia religious system is, therefore, a mixture of tribal and Hindu religious elements.

Concept of God: Bhagwan

The Bharias, like Gonds and the Hindu castes living in the neigh bourhood, believe that *Bhagwan* or *Parmatma* is the Supreme Being. He is god of all gods (*Sab devon ka deo*). He is almighty. He is the creater of the sun, moon and all life. In spite of this popular version, the Bharias do not seem to have a clear picture of *Bhagman* in their minds. They do not worship him in the manner of other gods and deities. They do not remember him regularly or even on ritual occasions. They do not offer him sacrifices with a view to appeasing him. Indeed, the *Bhagwan* regarded as the Supreme and all-powerful appears to have no direct influence on the day-to-day life of the Bharias. When asked what is *Bhagwan* like, Chintaman replied, "Eh, you should know and tell us. We do not know." And Jangal Singh remarked, *Akash* (sky), *Patal* (underworld), *Suraj* (sun), *Chand* (moon), and *Dharti* (earth) are also *roop* (forms) of *Bhagwan*. How would humans be able to live without them?" It would appear that *Bhagwan* is more of a philosophical concept than a supernatural being with some kind of anthropomorphic form. No Bharia has any prayers for *Bhagwan*, nor is he afraid that *Bhagwan* would make him ill. It is indeed the other gods and deities who play an important role in the Bharia life, and these are discussed here.

Baradeo

The highest tribal deity of the Bharia is *Baradeo*. This deity is often equated with *Mahadeo* or Lord Shiva of the Hindus, but many Bharias indicate that *Baradeo* is different from Shiva. The seat of *Baradeo* is always at the bottom of the *Saj* tree where an unhewn stone of Phalic shape is installed by a Bharia. No earthern platform is made, so that the sacred stone may be misplaced or lost. In case this happens another stone of similar shape is installed at the place of worship.

Though all the Bharias worship *Baradeo*, the worship is actually a family affair. Each family or a group of families related through agnatic bonds has its own place of *Baradeo* worship under a *Saj* tree. The *Baradeo* of Tidhu Bharia, for example, is at the *Saj* tree near the water reservoir from where the people of Rated village draw drinking water. Mehtar's *Baradeo* is situated near his own kitchen garden, not far away from his house.

Baradeo is worshiped twice a year: first in the month of *Ashada* and later during the *Dussehra*. The sacrifices of a goat or a red chicken was all that this high god received during the worship. *Baradeo* is worshiped by each family immediately after the *Bidri* right. The worship is performed by all brothers of a Bharia jointly. However, should a person begin to live away from his brothers, he may establish a separate shrine of *Baradeo* near a *Saj* tree. At the time of worship the *Bhumka* (Bharia priest) must be present. He prays to the deity and says, "*Maharaj* we are giving you these fowls and eggs. We are going to sow seeds in the *Bari*. You help us. We will sow seeds in the fields. We pray you to give us good crops. We cook our food in *handi* (earthen pot) and so keep our *handi* and *chattu* (laddle) safe. We should never fall short of our daily food. Allow our cattle to wander and live with the tigers. We pray to you that our cattle should return home safely and the tigers may go back to the forest. We pray to you for good health. We all should remain healthy in hands and legs. No disease should inflict us." The priest sacrifices the fowl and spills the blood on the stone of *Baradeo*. After this the fowl is moved to and fro and some water is sprinkled. This is called *Pani sarana* or "sprinkling of water" after which the fowl is roasted. Some *kutki* is cooked and the members eat the *bhat* (gruel) and chicken. After this they return home. At home they take water in a *lota*, and some turmeric, milk and a little cowdung, and sprinkle it in the house. An earthen lamp is lit and *Dhartimata* (mother earth) is worshipped first, and then the gods in the basket. With the offerings of eggs, coconut and dried dates the family gods are appeased and prayed. On behalf of Mehtar, Chinta and Bhondal the worship is done by Chintaman in his house. Thus one of the members among the agnates is the repository of the family deities and is also responsible for the worship of the *Baradeo* who brings goodwill and prosperity to the agnatic families. This worship is called *Navatari*. Unless this worship is done, the Bharias are afraid that they may be bitten by a snake, one of the cattle may die, or one may get a fatal wound from the axe.

Baradeo is honoured with similar worship before the Dussehra festival. The worship is termed *Aathi-navan*, meaning "eighth day" of the *Asvin* month which is considered auspicious for eating new grains. The Bharias say that the new grains are consumed even earlier, but a man in that case ought not to mix old and new grains during cooking and eating. It is only after the *Aathinavan* rite that the distinction of old and new cereals is brought to an end. Now old and new grains may be mixed freely and consumed.

Other Gods

Apart from *Baradeo* there are a large number of gods, both male and female, in the Bharia pantheon. A classification of Bharia deities, depending upon the nature and functions they perform, is shown below:

Village Gods: Each Bharia village has some sacred place for a few important deities. The most important among these deities is the *Mata* also called *Devimata* or *Kherekimata*. The *Mata* is represented by a stone near the *Kakai* tree. An earthen platform is made and the stone representing the *Mata* with a vermilion coating may be seen fixed in the centre. An iron trident about a foot high is fixed on the platform and is called *Khambha*. Many illnesses are believed to afflict the Bharias because of the anger of the *Mata*. The Bharias, therefore, worship her twice annually; once in the month of *Chaitra* and then before the Dussehra festival. It is for the village priest to arrange for the worship of the *Mata* by the village community. After the day has been fixed by the village elders, 25 to 30 paise are collected from each house for the purchase of coconuts, dry dates, jaggery, some *ghee* and a few limes. A small piece of cloth is required for offering to the *Mata* a *Jhandi* (small flag). The rite is performed in the morning hours and at least one male member from each Bharia family is required to attend to the worship. The *Bhumka* offers prayers to the *Mata* and begs her to keep the children and all persons healthy. He prays to her to keep all the village members free from cough, cold and fever and their cattle in good health. After prayers the offerings are made and the *prasad* is distributed to all who are present.

Apart from the two annual worships the *Mata* may actually be prayed and appeased at any time when a Bharia falls ill. According to the Bharias if the *Mata* takes the slightest offence, she spreads malaria and may also send them smallpox. When that happens the *Bhumka* is called in to appease the goddess with the offerings of water. He prays and begs for the patient's recovery by regularly going to the shrine of the *Mata*. This is believed to improve the patient's health. The Bharias say that *Mata* takes mercy upon them and allows the patient to recover. After the patient's recovery the *Bhumka* makes offerings of coconut or such other articles like a trident or a flag according to promises made. If a patient's condition is serious, the *Bhumka* while making offerings of water may promise two or more coconuts to the *Mata* instead of one. In all such cases the promisesare fulfilled as soon as the patient has recovered.

Muthua: Another village deity is *Muthua*. This is believed to be a male deity who looks after the welfare of the village community. The Bharias compare *Muthua* to a *Patel*, a *Mukadam* or a *Kotwar* who takes note of everything that happens in the village. *Muthua* is regarded as one of the escorts of *Mata* and is, therefore, worshipped with *Mata*, annually. In Rated village the shrine of *Muthua* is near the shrine of *Mata*. The Bharias of Rated village say that formerly the shrine lay below a *ber* tree which sheltered it. But several years ago the tree fell down and as a result the stone representing the *Muthua* had to be re-installed at the same place. Apart from the two worships during the year, *Muthua* may also be prayed and worshiped when a Bharia falls ill because, like the *Mata*, he is also believed to give the Bharias different kinds of illnesses. While she is believed to bring epidemic, he is believed to bring different kinds of fevers to individuals with whom he may get offended. The *Bhumka* comes to the shrine of *Muthua*, offers water to it after prayers, and promises to make offerings of coconut after the recovery of the patient. It is mainly the *Muthua* and the *Mata* who are appeased during common illnesses.

Jhiriya: *Jhiriya Mata* or the "Spring mother" is also an important deity. She is believed to be the "mistress" of drinking water and is believed to be responsible for the health and well-being of the Bharias. For Rated village the seat of the *Jhiriya Mata* lies near a small pit with a perennial source of water. She is worshipped during the month of *Magha*. Since her benevolence and mercy are deemed essential for the general well-being, the Bharias sacrifice a goat to honour this deity at least once in three to four years. The Bharias feel that if this is not done the *Jhiriya Mata* may feel that she is being neglected and hence make people ill.

Bhimsen—God of cultivation: The most important deity of cultivation whose benevolence the Bharias pray for good harvest is *Bhimsen*. He is not just a village god, since the annual *Bidri* rite held in his honour in the month of *Jyaistha* is jointly performed by Rated, Kaream and Dodipara which are Bharia villages and Bijadana and Thanakheda which are Gond villages. Thus the worship of *Bhimsen* is actually an expression of inter-community ritual performed by the Gonds and Bharias jointly who share common interests in cultivating fields lying inside and outside the vicinity of Patalkot.

Bhimsen is believed to be a very powerful deity who is master of the entire area of these villages including the forest. The shrine of *Bhimsen* lies outside Patalkot near its boundary wall. According to the Bharias *Bhimsen* controls the rains and if he remains unappeased he may cause a drought thus making it difficult for the Bharias to survive. It is believed that *Bhimsen* has a big *lashkar* (army) or a group of deities who serve him as his escort. The prominent among these are: *Bhasmasur*, *Sinwardeo*, *Dongardeo*, *Kalyandeo*, *Srideo*, *Baghdeo* and *Kudopen*. These forest deities are believed to be in perpetual attendance on *Bhimsen* and are jointly worshipped when sacrifices are made to *Bhimsen* annually.

Forest deities

Bhasmasur: This is believed to be a very powerful deity who must be worshipped along with *Bhimsen*. The Bharias believe that when *Bhasmasur* was born the entire world became dark. The Sun set and hid itself due to fear. It was then *Bhimsen* who, with his might, brought *Bhasmasur* under control. It was only after this that all other deities who had run away to sky and to land below the earth returned to their places. Since then *Bhasmasur* (described as a demon) stays as a loyal attendant of *Bhimsen*.

Sinwardeo: *Sinwardeo* is believed to be a female deity and queen of the forest. The Bharias say that *Dongardeo* and *Srideo* are her brothers and along with the sister *Sinwardeo* form escort to *Bhimsen*. *Sinwardeo's* attendants are believed to be *Baghdeo* and *Baghdano*. *Sinwardeo* and *Dongardeo* move together in company of their attendants. They keep tigers and panthers under control. These deities of the forest are responsible for protecting cattle from the wild animals. If they are sympathetic to the people they send the wild animals away from the heards of cattle. If a tiger kills a cow, the Bharias conclude that *Sinwardeo* and *Dongardeo* are offended. Killing of cattle by wild animals is regarded merely as a game of *Sinwardeo* who is believed to direct *Baghdeo* or tiger god to kill the cattle. *Sinwardeo* is believed to reside under a rock on the hilltop called *Buduldiya* that lies on the western hill running beyond Kaream and Rated villages. No Bharia ever goes to this rock for worship. The offerings may, however, be made at some place near the house or during the annual *Bidri* rite near the shrine of *Bhimsen*.

Ghurlapat: It is a small deity who is believed to ride a horse and go about according to the dictates of *Bhimsen*. The Bharias believe that if one were to come on his way he may fall ill and may not recover until he has propitiated him. *Bhimsen* may send pests through *Ghurlapat* to the fields of the Bharias.

Household deities

Apart from the gods described above the Bharias also have a set of household deities called *Deokholi* gods contained in a basket. The basket is kept in the house of one of the agnatic male members of the lineage and the families are expected to worship the deities periodically. These deities are said to be seven in number but in many cases their number varies. Their names and the material of which they are made is as follows:

Budhi Dayi — This deity, also called *Budhi Bhavani*, is represented by an image made of a

	thin sheet of silver. This is made by a gold or silversmith and is in the shape of a big *Tabeej* talisman. She is believed to keep the diseases away and protect the house.
Khodia-Khatarpal	*Khodia-Khatarpal* are believed to be two brothers, the latter being the elder though the name is taken after Khodia. These are represented by two rectangular pieces of wood of *mundi* tree. The pieces are identical but the person who worships these gods periodically knows them both by name.
Thakurdeo	This god is represented by a small image made of iron.
Narangdeo	Narangdeo or Narayandeo is also represented by an image made of iron. *Narayandeo* is the sun god.
Dhanabai	*Dhanabai* is believed to be the goddess *Lakshmi*. She is the goddess of wealth and prosperity. Its image is made of iron. The Bharias are unable to explain as to why the goddess of wealth is represented by iron and not by a costlier metal like silver.
Saklai	*Saklai* also called, *Sakarai* is a deity in the form of an iron chain or iron links fixed to secure the doors.
Dulhadeo	Literally the bride groom god is made of a piece of iron. In the spiritual world he is regarded as the master of the house.

In addition to these gods and goddesses there are also a number of other gods whose names are taken during the worship of these deities, even if not all Bharias keep their images in the Deokholi baskets. Along with *Dhanabai* the name of *Dhan Thakur* is also mentioned. *Adhartuni* is believed to be a god "who acts as the base in domestic life in the same manner as a forked post supports the main beam of the house." Then there is the *Panda* or worshipper, the representation of the *Bhumka* whose main job is believed to be to worship the gods. *Bhura Bhagat* is regarded as some kind of a saint. *Durga* or *Durga Bhavani* and *Mahadeo* along with the *trisul* or trident are obviously Hindu gods who have also been accepted in the Bharia pantheon of the domestic deities. Nevertheless the main gods and goddesses of *Deokholi* are only those who are represented with images of wood and iron.

Ajya ka Chowtra: Near one of the houses of the agnatic male members is a small platform which the Bharias call *Ajya ka Chowtra*, or grandfather's sitting place. The Bharias believe that this platform is the seat of the great grandfathers and grandmothers who, while they live in the land of the Dead, still continue to have association with this world. Since the Bharias are afraid of the return of the dead to this land, they worship them after the Holi festival so that they are appeased and they bless the family. A coconut or a cock, eggs and five small *luchis* cooked in some oil are offered to the ancestors. The worship is named *Tiharu*. The person worshipping the ancestors' shrine says, "we are making to you these offerings. We are giving to you a cock. Now remain happy for 12 months. Look after us and our children. Manage our affairs well."

Supernatural beliefs

The Bharias have a number of magical and supernatural beliefs. These beliefs have come down to them from the days of their forefathers and are persistent to this day. These beliefs can be grouped into a few categories, namely: beliefs related to dreams, beliefs related to names, beliefs related to journeys and beliefs related to the "evil eye."

Beliefs related to dreams: The Bharias believe that dreams forecast future happenings, and the common belief is that "if you see good things in a dream, it is likely to bring some kind of misfortune." After a dream, a man or woman discusses it with the family members and other relatives and friends; and then they interpret it according to their faith and knowledge. But no further action is taken to avert the danger of a possible misfortune except that no journey should be undertaken after a dream that forebodes illness or some other evil. The Bharias were reluctant to give details of the dreams they had seen within the month, or such other dreams as they could remember, "We are afraid," said Premlal Bhumka, "because if one of us narrates his dream it may still come to have its effect." However, the Bharias indicated a few dreams along with the meanings they attached to them. If a man sees in a dream a horse or many horses, it is a bad omen. Though it is all right to see a horse in day-to-day life, in a dream it indicates illness because some of the spirits ride this animal. To see a road or a track in a dream is also bad and if one finds himself walking on the road in rain, it indicates that he would suffer from some illness. If one sees in a dream that he is walking through a forest or guarding his crops in rain he takes it that he would fall ill. On the other hand if in a dream one sees the flowing water and the making of a bund to stop the flow, he takes it that he would recover from illness or overcome some kind of difficulty. A forest-fire seen in a dream is indicative of bright sunshine.

Beliefs related to names: If children do not survive in a family, it is considered that such misfortunes might have occurred due to good names given to them. The spirits are believed to be fascinated by good names and, if they repeatedly hear such names, they try to "take away the child." Such names as Bhangi, Mehtar or Chamru are significant in this context. Chamru meaning Chamar or Cobbler was the name given to late Deochand's son. The boy was healthy and handsome and the parents decided to give him this name so that the spirits do not take note of him. Chamru gave his two sons derogatory names, "Bhangi" and "Mehtar", in the belief that if they were called by sweeper's name they would live long. While this is mostly true of boys, girls are also often given such names as "Kali" meaning black, "Papadi" meaning crust, "Patti" meaning leaf, and "Hini" meaning thin. The Bharias say that in most cases insignificant, derogatory or meaningless names keep off evil eyes and the children lead a long life.

Good and bad omens related to journeys: Belief in good and bad omens related to the commencement of a journey is widely prevalent among the Bharias. The success or failure of a journey much depends on the type of omen. Thus if a man while coming out of his house for a journey sees a woman with a pitcher full of water, he believes that his journey would be successful and that he would be able to complete the work for which he was going. So is the sight of a cow with a calf which is held by them to be a good omen. On the other hand, if one finds a person carrying a bundle of wood or a log, it is considered an ill omen. Though a Bharia would not care if he saw a monkey, he would in all probability abandon his journey if a monkey or a snake crossed his path. Similarly the Bharias believe that appearance and twittering of *sui* bird is also an ill omen. If a man hears its twitter, he tries to avoid hearing or seeing it while going on a journey.

The Bharia believes in and is scared of the effect of casting of an evil eye, *nazar lagna*. In former days, they claim, there were persons among them who could dry up a tree or the whole field overnight by casting an evil eye. They say that, fortunately, the craft has not been passed on to the present generation. When a child falls sick constantly, or a cattle dies or even some field dries up they attribute it to the ill effects of an evil eye. The ill effect is removed by the *Bhumka*.

Belief in evil spirits: An evil spirit is either a *bhoot* or a *churd* to the Bharia, the former being a male and the latter a female. These spirits are believed to be the spirits of people who die an unnatural death and, therefore, are also referred to as *Shaitan*. Such spirits haunt the forests, river banks and shadowy recesses, and should a Bharia by chance go to one of these places, he is most likely to be afflicted by some ailment. The symptoms include high temperature and sapping up of the vitals finally resulting in death. Among the spirits, *Matiya* is the most powerful.

The *Bhumka* may try to cast off the evil spirit from a person but, it is believed, he usually fails, resulting in the death of the affected person.

If the sylvan deities are unsatisfied they may command a tiger to kill the person concerned. The Bharias believe that a tiger would not attack and kill a man except when the forest deities direct it to do so.

Role of Bharia pantheon in their socio-economic life

The foregoing account shows how much the life of a Bharia is guided by their religious beliefs and belief in the pantheon. The Bharia pantheon affects the economic prosperity, social life and even fertility in women.

Bharia pantheon vis-a-vis social life: Marriage and death are the two landmarks in the life of a Bharia. Birth of a child is a happy occasion, yet it is not celebrated due to the fear of spirits, who may take note and "take away" the child. This is warded off by a brief rite in which a black thread is tied loosely round the limbs, the waist and the neck of a baby. On the fifth day a small purificatory rite is performed in which the parturient woman, after a bath, ceremoniously attends to a feast which may be partaken by the other female folk. This feast establishes the child's arrival among the group of relatives in the social sense.

The Bharia believes that every human being is tied to *Bhagwan* or *Baradeo* with a cord of life. When the cord breaks the man loses his life and dies. *Mari-garai* is the term for death.

The causes of death are differentiated; death due to old age or a prolonged illness is considered natural. All others are, therefore, unnatural and may be the handiwork of evil spirits. *Matiya*, a *bhoot*, is largely responsible for death as he "takes away" the person. He kills both human beings and animals. Death is also attributed to *gun* (witchcraft). An affected person may not know that he is influenced by *gun*: it is only the *Bhumka* who can know of it. The *Bhumka*, in order to ward off the spirit, chants magical formulae, promises the ghost eggs, chicken, coconut and prays for the patients' recovery. If the ghost leaves him he may survive, otherwise he dies.

The priests

There are three types of priests among the Bharias: the *Bhumka*, the *Padihar* and the *Deo-chads*. The *Bhumka* of the village is responsible for the annual rites held to venerate the *Mata* and other deities. He is also responsible for the *Bidri* rite which is described in the following pages. In illness, at the first instance, it is the *Padihar* who is called to attend the patient. A *Padihar* usually chants incantations while holding grains in his right hand and uttering the name of the particular deity supposed to be responsible for the illnens. He throws some grains on the floor and then counts them. According to the number being odd or even, the deity responsible for causing illness is ascertained. The process is called *Kanuka beenana* or *Dana-beenana*. This done, the *Padihar* goes to the concerned shrine with a *lota* of water. Tying part of his turban around his neck and standing on one leg, he usually prays to the deity in the following words:

> See my neck in the death noose, my feet in shackles. I am praying to you holding water. Be pleased and leave the patient . . . . Listen to my *araj* (*prayer*).

Ritual and economic life

Economic prosperity of the Bharia depends upon agriculture and here again the deities are believed to play a vital role. *Bhimsen*, the god of rains, controls the clouds loaded with water. "If he becomes angry", the Bharias would say, "the clouds may float away without allowing a drop of water to fall in their valley. Even if there are rains, the danger of pests is always present which, they believe, is sent by *Bhimsen* to their fields through *Ghurlapat*, a deity who is believed to ride a horse.

Feasts, fasts and festivals

Though the system of *dahiya* cultivation has been abandoned and settled agriculture is practised by the Bharias, yet the most important economic rite related to *dahiya* cultivation has been retained. This rite is called *Bidri* and is performed in the month of *Jyaishta*

The rite is performed in honour of *Bhimsen*, the god of cultivation. A few days before the rite is performed a sum of 50 paise or a *paili* of grains is collected from each Bharia house. With such collection or purchases of such articles of worship as coconuts, dried dates, turmeric, yarn, some oil, etc., on the day decided by the *Bhumka*, young men carry these things to the shrine of *Bhimsen* where they await the arrival of the priests before the morning breaks. The *Bhumka* alongwith his assistant has to perform small rites to *Jhiriamata* and other village deities. The people who have retained a bison horn since long blow it frequently in the village as well as near the shrines of *Bhimsen* at small intervals on the *Bidri* day.

After arriving near the shrine of *Bhimsen*, the *Bhumka* makes a small leaf hut and installs two small images of *Neora-Neori* carved out of wood. The images are coloured with turmeric and tied together with yellow yarn. During the rite, Premlal Bhumka was assisted by another priest named Chintaman Bharia, a man fairly well-versed in religious incantations. The *Bhumka* made prayers to *Bhimsen* and to a number of deities associated with him, particularly to the *Neora-Neori* who were also symbolically married. After the prayers were over, *Bhimsen* was offered eggs and chickens. Offerings of chicken were also made to *Baghdeo* and other deities, who were similarly prayed to keep the Bharias in good health and free from dangers of the forest.

It was well in the afternoon that the Gonds and Bharias began to come one by one, or in small groups. As soon as one came, he gave the *chappatis* brought by him to a man of his tribe for the feast, and placed the basket containing grains, iron rings of the *bukkhar* and ropes of bullocks at a convenient place. He approached the small hut near the shrine of *Bhimsen* with folded hands and bowed before the *Neora-Neori* and *Bhimsen*, praying for good crops. He would keep a few coins near the shrine, and then the priest and others would meet him turn by turn, after which he would receive some coconut as *prasad*.

In the evening the Bharia and Gond women came wearing clean *saris*, blouses and ornaments, and started gossiping and joking. Then the *Bhumka* requested the men to assemble near a patch of land (about 3′×4′) which had been cleared to represent a *dahiya* field. Some grass had been placed and no sooner the priest had offered prayers to *Bhimsen,* then he set fire to the grass. After the grass had burnt a little, the ashes were scattered by the crowd of farmers who now began to move the iron rings all over the patch of land, shouting *hirr...hirr...chal beta chal* (go...son...go) as though the bullocks were ploughing the land. While they did this they sprinkled the grains on the *dahiya* patch, and since there were no rains, artificial rains had to be created. Young men who had brought water in brass vessels sprinkled some of it on the people and the *dahiya* plot. The women laughed as some of their men got wet. It was only by chance that a patch of black cloud hid the sun, and though there were no rains the environment became cool and comfortable.

The Bharias and Gonds thought this to be a good augury and felt that *Bhimsen* had listened to their prayers after all, and that there would be rains at the appropriate time. The farmers of both tribes put the remaining grains on a piece of cloth which had been spread by the *Bhumka*. This collection was to be shared by the two priests later on.

While the *Bidri* rite was being performed, the Bharias made a fire and put the flesh of fowls to boil. Now the men and women sat in separate lines and groups for the feast, the members of one clan joining their own. Leaf plates made by Bharias were placed in front of them, and the chappatis, cooked lintels, and chicken was served to all. The chicken was too little for the large number of men and women, but all of them shared whatever was available and were satisfied.

Once the feast was over, the women stood in a circle. They sang songs and the necessary rhythm was provided by a Bharia young man wearing a large white turban playing the single membrane *timki* with two wooden sticks.

Apart from the *Bidri* rite there are no economic ceremonies in the nature of community or intercommunity worship. If the rains are meagre, they all suffer in common. But, if the pests attack one's fields, one may perform a small rite individually to appease the offended deity or deities.

Feasts serve more than one function. Every feast involves invariably an offering to the deity which, psychologically speaking, satisfies the Bharia. It also means the assembly of relatives who may not otherwise find time for a get-together. Such assemblies often discuss and decide disputes and settle marriages. But apart from social and economic and ritual fulfilments, a feast is an occasion for merriment and enjoyment. It is not uncommon to find some eldery persons to stay on with the host for more drinks. Liquor occasionally, however, leads to quarrels though the Bharias try to avoid unpleasant scenes in a feast.

The Bharias do not appear to have any festival which is indigenous or their own. Due to several centuries of contact with the Gonds and the Hindus of the plains they have taken to some of the Hindu festivals such as *Hori* (Holi), *Diwari*, (Deepawali) and *Rakhi* (Rakshabandhan). Since when these festivals came to be celebrated by the Bharias is difficult to say, because "as far as their memory goes, they have always been celebrating them."

Holi is celebrated in the month of *Phalgun* and in the usual Hindu manner. Almost every adult Bharia brings wood during the fortnight preceding Holi, and stacks near the place of burning. On the day of burning *Holi*, the firewood is properly piled and the *Bhumka* sets fire to it. Unlike the traditional Hindu belief, however, the Bharias believe that on the Holi day Ram and Laxman had killed Ravan and set fire to Lanka and burnt it down. They say that after every 12 months, Ravan becomes alive, and it shall continue to be so. As such, they would have to burn him in the *Holi* every year. The men and women who assemble to celebrate this festival dance to the rhythm of *timki*, while the fire blazes. The next morning, the *Bhumka* brings some ash and sprinkles on the houses to drive away disease. Bharias being poor cannot afford to procure much coloured powder, but they use some of it as well as *gulal*, or red ochre. On this day food is usually better than the usual food, and those who can afford may eat *luchis*, fried in oil or *ghee* with jaggery.

During *Dussehra* the Bharias worship the *Mata*, renew the vermilion marks on the stone image and offer her a new flag in a community worship. *Diwari*, or Deepawali follows Dussehra. Though Deepawali is the festival of lights, the Bharias associate it with the welfare of their cattle. For the entire village the *Bhumka* worships the village deities after which four to six *pailis* of grains are cooked in each house. Before this, cooked food is offered to the cattle, and cows are decorated with peacock feathers. In every house either the husband or the wife must observe fast to feed the cattle. The mouths of cows are washed, a lamp is lit and three or four paise are placed near the lamp. *Teeka* is done with rice to all cows, and later on to the men. After this the cooked food, usually *khichri*, or *luchis* fried in oil are offered to the cattle. Food for the family is cooked and this festival provides an occasion to eat some good food like *luchis* fried in oil or *ghee*. In the night one or more—up to seven—lamps are lighted and placed at different places inside and outside the house. Those who do not purchase *diyari* or earthen lamps, make small *diyari* with flour and light them with oil. Thus the Bharias celebrate Deepawali, and in this celebration they associate their cattle too. After the *Diwari*, *Holera Deo* is also worshipped. It is a small unoffensive deity of the graziers and is believed to protect the cattle from disease. The Bharias dance in honour of *Holera Deo*.

In the month of *Sawan* (Shravan) the Bharias celebrate Rakshabandhan. They ensure that their sisters and daughters come to their parental home for this festival and stay with their parents for some days. The girls bring *rakhi-phul*, a coloured yarn which they purchase from the bazar, to tie round the right wrists of their brothers. The brothers are in turn obliged to give their sisters some cloth and feed them well before they return to their husbands' homes. Young unmarried girls also tie *rakhi-phul* to their brothers and expect some clothes in return.

Bharia and Hinduism

For centuries the Bharias have lived with the Gonds under the influence of Hinduism. To the Bharia, Hinduism has meant substitution of old deities with the new, change in religious practices and beliefs, and introduction of certain new values in life. Turning to the Bharia deities, we find that *Bhagwan* is rather a philosophic concept than a deity in the real sense, and the Bharias attribute things and happenings to *Bhagwan* the same way as the common Hindu peasantry in India. The Bharias have also adopted the concept of fate, *Karma* or *Bhagya* and the commonest saying among them is "whatever is in *nasib* (fate) would befall one." Their *Baradeo* is often equated with *Mahadeo*, Lord Shiva, though the Bharias may have it in their mind that they are originally different. Yet we find a new synthesis, a tribalgod being replaced by a new deity of theHindu pantheon. Similarly *Mata* is referred to as *Gauri*, a name for *Parvati*, though in the tribal areas of the south, *Mata* is always associated with fury, epidemics and demons or disease. *Dhanbai* in her new form has become goddess Laxmi, though the name *Dhanbai* (Laxmi) itself might have been adopted from the Hindu pantheon. Again while *Narayandeo* (sun) is a deity of the Hindus, there are many deities such as *Baghdeo*, *Sinwardeo*, *Dongardeo* and *Gurlapat* which seem to be typically tribal. While some of the deities have received new names and are equated today with the Hindu gods and godesses, there are others which remain typically tribal. Another important change brought about by Hinduism is the change in rites and rituals.

Till some four decades ago the Bharias used to sacrifice a bullock for the journey of the dead, and in those days beef was freely eaten. Gonds did the same; but during the past few decades beef eating has been decried by the Gonds in the name of reform, therefore the Bharias too have abandoned cow slaughter. There are no Bharias who eat beef nowadays. The smaller kinds of sacrifices are also under change. Fewer goats and fowls are sacrificed to the deities, and the reason is not the comparative poverty of the Bharia, but a real shift from the traditional religious thought. Instead of sacrificing an animal or bird, they now offer the deities water, coconut and dried dates, though lime and jaggery as offerings to deities must be pretty ancient. The *Bhumka* is nowadays also referred to as *pujari*, the common name of the Hindu priests.

The adoption of Hindu festivals is yet another trait adopted by the Bharias as part of hyper-culturation. The Bharias, as has been noted, do not seem to have any of their own festivals, but the celebration of Holi, Diwali and Rakshabandhan brings joy to the village community. The *Bidri*, however, remains the typical Bharia rite, or a festival, if one wishes to call it, because there is the community feast and the dance.

Finally it may also be noticed that a number of other subtle religious elements have been borrowed by the Bharias from the Hindus. In one or two houses of the Bharias copies of the Ramayan are found, which are occasionally read by neo-literate

Bharia boys. On certain occasions, the Bharias may assemble to hear recitations from the Ramayan. They also observe Holi to celebrate victory of Ram and Laxman. There are many who know that some of the well-to-do among the Hindus and also among the Gonds occasionally invite a priest to recite the *Satyanarayan Katha*. A Bharia knows practically all important deities of the Hindu pantheon, such as Siva, Ganesh, Laxmi, and such legendary figures of the Mahabharat as Kauravas and Pandavas, or of the Ramayan such as Ram, Laxman, and Sita. To observe a fast is something different from the traditional Bharia religious philosophy, yet during Diwali they observe a fast until they have fed their cows ritually and worshipped them.

These and many other changes that are taking place in the Bharia life have transformed the old religious ideas to a great extent, and no wonder that the Bharias have returned themselves as Hindus during the last census.

6

EXTENT OF CHANGE

IN THIS chapter an attempt has been made to highlight the areas of change and also to indicate the relative incidence of change in a few selected culture traits in order to bring home the extent and direction of change taking place in the Bharia culture. For this, two points of time, that is, 1940 and 1970, werechosen. The traits selected for the study broadly relate to: Material culture and economic life, Social life, Religious life, and Leadership.

These traits, it is considered, would represent not only the broad spectrum of the various aspects of the Bharia culture, but also provide a basis for the study of impact as a result of contact with the outside world. It is often believed that culture traits, like religious beliefs and certain aspects of marriage, fall under "core culture traits" which are not easily amenable to change either through evolution or as a result of contact with external forces. On the other extreme are traits like material culture, economic pursuits and leadership which form "peripheral culture traits" easily amenable to change owing to external contacts. In selecting the culture traits, for studying the dynamics of change both types have been taken into account.

Let us now examine each one of these broad culture traits and try to understand the extent of change, if any, that has taken place.

Material culture and economic life

For the purpose of this study four aspects were selected under material culture. They included: (i) dress of men and women, (ii) hair-style of men and women, (iii) house and household articles for cooking, storing and sleeping, and (iv) implements used for economic pursuits like hunting fishing and farming.

(i) Dress of men and women

Under this aspect, head-dress, upper garments and lower garments, used by both men and women; were taken into account. A total of 24 families were intensely interviewed[1] to find out the use of dress in 1940s and 1970s using the genealogical method. The results of the inquiry are shown in Table 8.

TABLE 8: **Typology of dress used in 1940s and 1970s**

Typology	Sex	No. using in 1940s	No. using in 1970s
(i) Head-dress			
Chindhi	M	8	3
Pagri	M	16	18
Cap	M	—	1
Bare head	M	—	2
(ii) Upper garments			
Bandi	M	22	7
Shirt	M	1	16
Jacket	M	—	1
Bare body	M	1	—
Angia	F	12	—
Polka	F	11	8
Blouse	F	1	16
(iii) Lower garments			
Langoti	M	4	1
Pancha	M	13	5
Dhoti	M	7	18
Patta	F	9	1
Sendri	F	15	23

Head-dress: Table 8 brings out the extent of persistence and change in respect of the use of various dresses used by men and women over three decades. Out of the three types of head-dress used by males such as *chindhi*, *pagri* and cap, *pagri* was the predominent (16 out of 24) head-dress of the males in 1940s. *Chindhi*, a cruder variety of *pagri* (turban) using a smaller piece of cloth, was used by eight persons out of 24 indicating its lesser popularity. Use of cap was not prevalent during those days.

Against this, in 1970s[2] 18 persons of the sample used *pagri*, three used *chindhi* and one used cap as head-dress. While more and more people use *pagri*, *chinddi* users are shrinking. Usage of cap as head-dress by the males is the result of contact with the outside world. In this area caps are worn by the political elite, village headman and also the more well-to-do. The use of cap in this area started mainly after the country gained Independence. Permeation of political consciousness due to increased outside contact, therefore, is perhaps the main reason for the change from *pagri* to "cap" as a head-dress.

For the married Bharia male, it is imperative to have his head covered. This custom was invariably followed in the past. It was reported that every male married member used some kind of head-dress in 1940s. This custom is undergoing change today. Now it appears that although they attach importance to wearing of some head-dress it is no taboo if someone does not wear it. In the sample, we find two people (of the younger generation) who do not wear any head-dress, indicating the direction of change that is taking place among the Bharia, particularly in the younger generation as far as the head-dress is concerned.

Upper garments: Two types of upper garments for the males, namely, *bandi* (a sleeveless jacket) and shirt, were reported to be in vogue during 1940s. In 1970s, however, besides the above two, *jacket* (an upper modern garment similar to the bush-shirt) is also reported to be used. Only 23 persons reported using any kind of upper garment in 1940s. One person reported that nothing was being used. Out of the 23, 22 reported using *bandi* and one used shirt. Against this in 1970s *bandi* users came down to seven, shirt users went up to 16 and one reported using jacket

This shows that use of modern garments by the male members is on the increase indicating a definite change from the use of traditional garments. In 1940s there were at least a few persons who did not use any upper garment but now there is none in that category.

As regards females, three types of upper garments were reported during 1940s. *Angia*, kind of bodice which covers the bosom and is fastened at the back with strings, was used by the majority as is revealed from the sample. Eleven out of 24 reported using *polka*, an improved version of *angia*. It was also reported that one used the modern blouse.

In 1970s, on the other hand, none was reported using *angia* whereas *polka* is still used by eight cases and blouse users have increased and are in a majority.

This clearly shows that there is a definite trend of change towards the modern dress, both in the case of males and females. This could be due to a variety of reasons such as contact, economic prosperity, interaction, etc.

Lower garments: The male members among the Bharia used three types of lower garments, namely, *langoti* (a strip of cloth used to cover the private parts), *pancha* (loincloth) and *dhoti*. In 1940s, four used *langoti*, 13 used *pancha* and seven *dhoti*, out of the 24 interviewed.

In 1970s, it was reported that the *langoti* and *pancha* users went down to one and five respectively, while *dhoti* users increased to 18.

If we try to arrange the three types of male lower garments in a gradation scale as per their evolution, the *langoti*, the *pancha* and the *dhoti* fall in that order. It is clear from this that there is a definite change from the traditional to the modern.

The females on the other hand were reported using two types of lower garments, namely, *patta* and *sendri* in 1940s. The *patta* is a type of bleached coarse *sari* with a narrow border and *sendri* a coloured *sari* with a broad border. Both are worn in the Maharashtrian style. In 1940s, nine cases of the sample were using *patta* and 15 *sendri*. Today the *sendri* users have risen to 23 whereas the *patta* users of the same sample have come down to one.

A comparative analysis of the dress pattern of the males and females, in 1940s and 1970s, shows that the trend of change is towards the modern types of dresses. At the same time, it could also be seen that use of some of the traditional types of dress persist with the Bharias. If one examines the correlation betwaen the age and the type of dress used, it is revealed that the persistence is more in the older generation whereas the change is perceptible in the case of younger generation.

The rate of change is fast in the case of the dress of men and women. The most important factor responsible for this appears to be contact, though limited, of the Bharias with the outside world. The Chindi market plays a prominent part in this. Persistence of the traditional dress, on the other hand, is on the decrease. In other words the change in material culture in terms of dress of men and women is comparatively faster as the same falls under the peripheral culture traits which are easily amenable to change owing to external contact.

(ii) Hair-style of men and women

Decoration of body is one of the characteristic features of all primitive communities. Among the males and the females two types of hair decoration are observed. Typology and incidence in the two different types as revealed by the 24 case studies are shown in Table 9.

TABLE 9: **Typology and incidence of hair decoration**

Typology	Sex	No. using in 1940s	No. using in 1970s
Full cutting	M	16	2
Half cutting	M	8	22
Bun	F	24	11
Tassel	F	—	13

It is apparent from Table 9 that full cutting (in which the whole hair is cropped) was the predominant pattern of hair-style among the males in 1940s. The other type, namely, half cutting (modern hair cropping) was resorted to by eight cases only during that period. In 1970s, on the other hand, males resorting to "full cutting" dwindled to two cases in the sample whereas those liking "half cutting" increased considerably.

Preference for the modern type of hair-style among the Bharia males is apparent. The case studies also reveal that the few males who continued full cutting belonged to the older generation and those who resorted to half cutting mostly belonged to the younger generation.

Bun and tassel are the two types of hair-styles followed by the famale folk. In the former case, the bunch of hair is rolled into a bun-like pattern whereas in the latter the lock of hair is plaited and decorated with cloth ribbons of different colours. In 1940s all the female reported using the "*bun*" style whereas in 1970s, 13 cases reported "tassel" style and 11 continued the bun style. In terms of change, it could be noticed that more and more females are resorting to plaiting of the lock of hair, which incidentally is the hair-style prevailing in the surrounding areas. This is another instance of borrowing of culture traits from the people living around them. At the same time, there is persistence in the hair-style as could be seen from Table 9. The traditional hair-style is followed more by the elderly women.

(iii) House and household articles

For the purpose of analysis three types of household articles, namely, (i) articles used for cooking and serving, (ii) articles used for storage, and (iii) articles used for sleeping, are taken into account.

Articles used for cooking: Under this item, information regarding three groups were collected. The cooking utensils used on hearth are *handi* (an earthen vessel), *khapri* (an earthen pan to make chappatis) and *tawa* (a circular piece of iron used for making chappatis).

Articles used for serving food and water: Under this fall *pathal* (leaves stitched together in the shape of a plate), *thali* (a brass plate), *lota* (a small brass container used for transferring water) and *glass* (metal tumbler for drinking water). (see Table 10).

TABLE 10: **Incidence of use of household articles**

Articles used	No. using in 1940s	No. using in 1970s
For cooking and serving		
Handi	24	24
Khapri	24	12
Tawa	1	12
For serving food and water		
Pathal	6	1
Thali	22	24
Lota	22	24
Glass (metal tumbler)	—	8

Articles used for transferring food: These consist of *dhodi* (a circular shallow wooden vessel), *chatawa* (a large wooden spoon), *tumba* (shell of a kind of gourd used for transferring water), *karchali* (flat iron laddle) and *chamach* (metal spoon). Table 11 indicates the incidence as was observed in the 24 cases.

TABLE 11: **Incidence of use of articles for transferring food**

Articles used	No. using in 1940s	No. using in 1970s
For transferring food		
Dhodi	18	16
Chatawa	24	24
Thumba	24	24
Karchali	—	13
Chamach	—	1

For preparing rice gruel or similar other foodstuff *handi* was used by all the informants in 1940s. The use of *handi* is continued by all the informants even in 1970s, primarily due to its cheapness and also because of its utility. The earthen *khapri* to make *chappatis* was used in all cases during 1940s whereas today only half of them are reported using the same. In 1940s, only one case was reported of using *tawa* besides *khapri*. As against this, half of the informants reported using *tawa* in 1970s, while the rest continue to bake chappatis in the *khapri*.

Originally, *pattal* (leaf plate) was the only article used for serving food. In 1940s, however, six persons of the sampleused *pattal* exclusively for serving food. Today, however, only one is reported using *pattal* for this purpóse. *Thali* (metal plate), as a utensil for serving food, was predominant even during 1940s. Then 22 reported using *thali*. In 1970s, however, all the informants reported using *thali*. *Lota* users even in 1940s accounted for a majoriiy of 22 out of 24. Today, all the informants use *lota*. Glass (metal tumbler) users, for drinking water, today are eight against none in 1940s.

For transferring food 18 of the informants used *dhodi* in 1940s. In 1970s the number of *dhodi* users came down to 16. *Chatawa* was being used to transfer food by all the informants in 1940s and the same trend is continuing. The use of *thumba* to transfer water was resorted to by all the 24 informants in 1940s and, even today, all of them use it. *Karchali*, the flat iron laddle, was not in vogue in 1940s. Today, more than half of them use it to transfer cooked food. *Chamach*, the metal spoon, was unheard of in 1940s. Today, one of the informants, at least, reported using it.

Storing utensils

Information regarding two categories of storing utensils has been collected—one for storing water and the other for grains.

Utensils used for storing water: *Madka* (large earthen pitcher), *ghagra* (large brass pitcher) and *ghagri* (small brass pitcher) are the three different types of utensils used for storing water (see Table 12). *Madka* was the favourite vessel in 1940s accounting for 23 of the informants. Today, however, only 12 of the informants are reported to be using it. *Ghagra* users were very few, say, four, in 1940s. Today a large number of informants (20) use *ghagra* for storing water. Water is carried from the water source, either in a small earthen pitcher or in a *ghagri*. Its users for carrying water in 1940s were negligible, only one informant reported using it. As against this, in 1970s 12 of the informants reported using it.

TABLE 12: **Incidence of use of containers**

Article used	No. using in 1940s	No. using in 1970s
For Storing water		
Madka	23	12
Ghagra	4	20
Ghagri	1	12
For storing grains		
Dulha or Bakhra	23	22
Kothi	3	5
Madka	1	1

Containers used for storing grain: *Dulha* or *bakhra* (bamboo granary), *kothi* (earthen granary) and *madka* (large earthen pitcher) are the different containers used for storing grain. *Dulha* or *bakhra* users in 1940s accounted for 23 informants whereas in 1970s 22 of them reported using this type of container. *Kothi* being an expensive container is used only by those who can afford. In 1940s only three were reported using this type of container whereas in 1970s the number rose to five. One informant has continued using *madka* as a container to store grain since 1940s.

Material used for sleeping

Information regarding material used for sleeping purpose was also collected from the 24 households. (see Table 13).

It would be seen from Table 13 that there is not much change in the use of various articles for sleeping purposes. *Pancha* (a small *dhoti*) was used by 11 informants in 1940s as against none today. *Dhoti* was used by seven of them in 1940s whereas today it is used by eight. *Chatai* and *chadar* are used by a very few people,

The former accounted for three in 1940s as against four today. In the case of the latter, one used in 1940s as against four today. Mattress was unknown in 1940s; today, however, one of the informants reported using this. Cot users are practically nil even today. Only one reported using this in 1970s whereas none was using it in 1940s. Almost everyone sleeps on the floor with or without using some kind of spread. This is true for both 1940s and today.

TABLE 13: **Incidence of use of sleeping material**

Material	No. using in 1940s	No. using in 1970s
Pancha	11	—
Dhoti	7	8
Chatai	3	4
Chadar	1	4
Mattress	—	1
Sleeping on floor	24	23
Sleeping on cots	—	1

Implements used for economic pursuits

Under this category implements used for hunting, fishing and farming are discussed.

Hunting implements: Four different types of hunting implements were reported to have been in use in 1940s. They were the gun (muzzle loader), *balam* (wooden spear), *kulhari* (axe) and *thunga* (spear). A total of eight persons out of 24 used all these weapons for hunting during 1940s. The rest did not report using any, because they did not hunt.

Against this, in 1970s, none reported using gun and *balam* whereas three reported using *kulhari* and one reported using *thunga*.

The change in the use of hunting implements is related to their economic pursuits. Now, shifting cultivation is not practised and therefore need for hunting has also considerably reduced.

Fishing implements: Both in 1940s and in 1970s, five types of fishing implements were reported to be in use—*bansi*, *jhanja*, *thali* (metal plate), *dhoti* (a piece of cloth) and *kumna* (fishing basket).

In 1940s all these implements were in vogue with the difference in the incidence of use. Most of the informants (23) reported using *thali* and *dhoti* for bailing out water. Nine reported using *jhanja* (a fishing trap) while five used *bansi* and one used *kumna*. In 1970s the incidence of use of *thali*, *dhoti* and *kumna* continued as previously, but the number of *bansi* users rose to eight but of *jhanja* came down to one.

Farming implements: Three kinds of farming implements were in vogue during 1940s: *kulhari* (a kind of axe), *hansiya* (a chopper) and *khanta* (wooden digging implement with an iron tip). All the 24 informants reported using all the three types of implements in different operations. It may be recalled that in 1940s all the households practised shfting cultivation and as such no other implement was required for the purpose.

Today the situation is different. The three above mentioned implements continue to be in use by 23 informants for different purposes other than shifting cultivation which is no more practised. Besides, in 1970s, three other implements came into use which are suitable for settled cultivation. They are: *hal* (plough), *bakhar* (a kind of plough with two pointed pegs) and *pirano* (as implement used for sowing). All the informants (save one who does not cultivate) used *hal* and *bakhar* whereas only seven reported using *pirano*. The reason for the small number of *pirano* users is due to the fact that the mode of sowing continues to be broadcasting for which no *pirano* is required.

In the case of farming implements change is more marked. Although shifting cultivation is no more practised, the Bharias continue to use the conventional implements for some purpose or the other. Change over to settled cultivation has, however, necessitated use of improved implements like *hal* and *bakhar*. An abstract of the typology of implements used for hunting, fishing and farming is given in Table 14 for purposes of comparison.

TABLE 14: **Typology and incidence of implements used for economic pursuits**

Typology	No. using in 1940s	No. using in 1970s
Hunting Implements		
Gun	3	—
Balam	1	—
Kulhari	3	3
Thunga	1	1
Fishing Implements		
Bansi	5	8
Jhanja	9	1
Thali	23	23
Dhoti	23	23
Kumna	1	1
Farming Implements		
Kulhari	24	23
Hansiya	24	23
Khanta	24	23
Hal	—	23
Bakhar	—	23
Pirano	—	7

Economic life

Aspects, such as type of cultivation, crop pattern, methods of food collection and dairy farming have been taken into account for collecting information on the economic life of the Bharias of Patalkot.

Type of cultivation: Three different types of cultivation can be identified among the Bharias in connection with their economic pursuits, either of the past or of the present. They are *dahiya* (slash-and-burn cultivation), settled or plough cultivation and *bari* (kitchen garden) cultivation.

Till recently the Bharias earned their living by the slash-and-burn cultivation. Being an inaccesible area they could clear whatever land they wanted and cultivated small millets and other hill produce. Things changed with the opening up of communications to the interior areas. The Government banned shifting cultivation in 1954 and dealt with the offenders very firmly. The Bharia, therefore, had no alternative than to resort to settled cultivation. The process, though not smooth, was accomplished without much disturbance in the socio-economic life of the people. Plough cultivation was in practice outside Patalkot and the Bharias were aware of it. In fact a few of them, like Chintaman Bharia, adopted this from their Gond neighbours living outside. They continued to raise in the settled fields the same products as when they practised shifting cultivation. *Bari* cultivation continues to be the same as before (in this a levelled plot of land behind the dwelling unit was used to raise some vegetables, millets and creepers).

The study of those who practised shifting cultivation reveals that in 1940s all resorted to this type of cultivation whereas today none does so. However, there has been no change in *bari* cultivation as all of them continue to practise it. Settled cultivation is of recent origin. Out of the 24 informants only 22 were agriculturists. The other two were daily wage owners. All the 22 were reported to be practising settled cultivation while none practised this type of cultivation in 1940s.

The change here is very perceptible. Shifting cultivation has become a thing of the past with all the Bharias. This has been brought about largely because of administrative action rather than an evolution in or diffusion of culture. As a result of this change, from shifting cultivation to settled cultivation, as is pointed out earlier, the technology of cultivation has also undergone changes. Now they use *hal* and *bakhar* drawn by bullock. In the former days when shifting cultivation was practised only simple tools like the axe and the dibbler were used.

Crop pattern: The change in type of cultivation has also brought about a change in the cropping pattern. Though some of the crops raised in the shifting cultivation fields are used even today, there is a definite change towards the use of improved variety of seeds such as *jagny*, paddy and wheat.

In the shifting cultivation fields cent per cent cultivators raised *bewar kutky* (small millet). In 1970s 22 of the informants cultivated *kutky* (same as *bewar kutky*) in their fields. *Madia* is another millet which was in vogue with 23 of the informants in 1940s. Today none practises *madia* cultivation. *Kang* was another popular crop in 1940s and 16 of the informants cultivated it. Today, however, none is reported to be raising this crop. *Kutky* and *dangra* are the two other crops raised by nine and four informants respectively in 1940s. In 1970s none has reported raising these two crops.

Besides *kutky*, which continues to be used since the shifting cultivation times, the other crops raised today include *kodo*, *jwar*, *chana*, *dhan*, *jagni* and wheat. These crops except *kutky* were never raised in 1940s when they resorted to shifting cultivation. Today, 21 of the informants raise *kodo*, five raise *jwar* and six of them wheat. Wheat and paddy are now additions to the crop pattern in the valley.

This obviously shows both continuity and change in the crop pattern of the Bharias. While they continue to grow *kutky* in the settled cultivation, they have also taken to some new crops like wheat and paddy.

Bari cultivation continues with the Bharias as before. In 1940s 23 of the informants raised *makka* in the kitchen garden. This trend continues even to this day. Another crop raised in 1940s was *barbatti* (a kind of peas). This was raised by 17 persons in 1940s and the same pattern still continuing. *Urad* (black gram) is another crop raised by two of the Bharia informants in 1940s. In 1970s none has reported having raised it.

Three other crops—wheat, *dhan* and *balhor*—were raised in the *bari* (kitchen garden) in 1970s. All the three were unknown in 1940s. The wheat and *balhor* raisers from 15 informants of the sample whereas two of them raised *dhan* in the *bari*.

A look at the cropping pattern in the kitchen garden indicates that although some of the crops raised in 1940s continue to be raised in 1970s, new additions are made to the existing list. This is mainly due to external contact.

An attempt was made to find out the use of chemical fertilizers by the Bharias. It was reported that none ever used chemical manure. They are apprehensive of the efficacy of chemical manure in raising agricultural crops. They also do not practice irrigation but depend on the rains. However, a microscopic minority of them sprinkle water in the *bari* when a crop like *dhan* or wheat is raised.

Modes of food collection

The three important modes of collection of food among the Bharias are hunting, fishing and gathering.

Hunting: As discussed earlier, due to scarcity of game in the area, hunting remains, by and large, a thing of the past. Even in 1940s not many people resorted to hunting as the main source of food. The weapons used were *ballam*, *thunga*, *kulhari* or a gun. The first three methods were used by most of the informants in 1940s. Gun was used for hunting by three of the informants in 1940s. In 1970s, only three reported using implements like *ballam*, *thunga* and *kulhari* while none reported using a gun. In fact, hunting is resorted to today only as a pastime and not as a source of food collection.

Fishing: Fishing continues to be an important source of food collection as in the past. Most of the informants continue to use the two traditional methods of catching fish: *machav* (poisoning) and *ulcha*. In *ulcha* the water is baled out and the fish caught with hand. Both these methods are followed even today. In 1940s five of the informants reported using *bansi* for fishing whereas in 1970s only one reported using the same. *Kumna*, used to carry fish, was used by almost all of them in the past whereas now only a few use it.

Fishing, therefore, continues to be an important source of food for the Bharias. As for as the technology of fishing is concerned, both persistence and change are discernible. In the former days, more people resorted to trapping whereas today this is not very much in vogue. Fishing by poisoning and by *ulcha* continues as in earlier days.

Gathering: Food collection from the forest is generally done by the female folk. They either dig out roots and tubers or gather forest produce like fruits and seeds. It continues to remain as a subsidiary source with all the families among the Bharias.

Dairy farming

Information on the types of animals kept and the products consumed and sold by the Bharias was also collected. From time immemorial the Bharia tribe is known for dairy farming. Almost every house possess some cattle, generally cows. In 1940s all the informants reported having kept cows. In 1970s, 23 of them reported that they owned cows. Buffalo keepers in 1940s accounted for seven of the informants whereas in 1970s only two of them possessed buffalo.

Dairy farming is a traditional occupation for the Bharias. They convert milk into ghee butter and sell the same either to the peddlers visiting the valley or in the weekly market. They very seldom use milk products, except butter milk which they wholely consume. There is no change in the habit of consuming buttermilk and butter. Sale of ghee as an economic persuit continues with the Bharia. In 1940s, all 24 of them reported that they sold *ghee*. In 1970s, only one did not sell *ghee*.

Dairy farming, therefore, gives no clue to the change which has taken place among the Bharias except in the price pattern. They keep the same type of cattle and they sell ghee to the outsiders.

Social life

With a view to studying the dynamics of change in the social life of the Bharias, some prominent customs regarding marriage have been selected. Under this category falls types of marriage, mode of acquiring a spouse, payment of bride price and practice of exogamy.

Types of marriage: Two types of marriage, namely, monogamy and polygyny prevail among the Bharias. In 1940s 21 out of 24 families interviewed reported the type of marriage as monogamous. Those reporting polygynous marriage in 1940s were three. As against this in 1970s, 21 of the sample reported practice of monogamy. The polygyny practitioners have come down to one. Two of the informants, all unmarried, considered both monogamy and polygyny as the norm.

Thus it may be seen that the concept of having one spouse

still continues with the Bharia. The incidence of practising polygyny has come down. This they attributed to the income of the families, and felt that unlike in olden days when they could afford to look after more than one wife, today it was with difficulty that they could provide all the necessities of one wife. Another reason for this phenomenon is that while in former days they wanted more hands to accomplish the arduous task of shifting cultivation covering more area, today they needed less working force. The usual pattern among the neighbouring tribe, the Gonds, is also monogamy. Although among the Bharias the monogamy pattern, by and large, continues, the trend for polygyny type of marriage has fallen considerably. The present trend of the mixed type of marriage is, perhaps, a transition from polygyny to monogamy.

Mode of acquiring spouse: Three different modes of acquiring spouse are reported during 1940s. They are: *lamjhana* (marriage by service), arranged type and *bithalna* (a secondary union after the death of the husband regularised by the consent of the Panchayat). Out of these, arranged marriages were reported by 16 informants in 1940s whereas *lamjhana* by seven and by one *bithalna*. It is claimed that *bithalna* was the common mode among the Bharias in the olden days although only one case was found in the sample. In 1970s no case of *bithalna* was reported indicating that this method of acquiring spouse is no more in vogue. Arranged type of marriage was reported by 14 informants whereas seven reported *lamjhana*. Three of the informants (the unmarried ones) considered that any of the type mentioned above was acceptable to any other.

A close look at the information on the mode of acquiring spouse indicates that the arranged type of marriage, although continues as a norm, its incidence is on the decrease. The *lamjhana* type continues to persist as in 1940s. It is interesting to note that the *bithalna* type has altogether vanished because of the contact with outside world. Now it is felt that *bithalna* is "uncivilized" and should not be resorted to. Those reported "any type" are youngsters with secular outlook. To sum up, there is not much change in the mode of acquiring spouse among the Bharias although, owing to their contact with the outside world, they in their anxiety to project a better image do not like to resort to *bithalna*, a custom which is looked down upon.

Payment of bride price: Payment of bride price is a characteristic feature of primitive communities. The different customs of acquiring a spouse is very much related to the payment of bride price. Information regarding the payment of bride price and regarding marriages without payment of bride price shows that in 1940s, 16 informants reported having paid bride price while the rest did not. The position in 1970s is not very different; fourteen informants reported having paid bride price. Three of the informants who are not married indicated that they liked both the types.

A discussion on the payment of bride price can be had only in the light of the mode of acquiring a spouse. In the *lamjhana* type of marriage there is no question of paying bride price because the *lamjhana* (son-in-law) works in the house of the girl in lieu of payment of bride price. In the arranged type of marriage, on the other hand, one can have the hand of the bride only if he pays the bride price. So the number reporting payment of bride price will be the same as that reporting arranged mode of acquiring a spouse. To sum up, the incidence of change in the payment of bride price has been very little.

Practise of exogamy: The two forms of exogamy discussed here are the clan-exogamy and village-exogamy.

In 1940s, cent per cent clan-exogamy was reported and none reported having practised clan endogamy. In 1970s, on the other hand, 21 reported practising clan exogamy. The rest of the informants were still unmarried, and although forward looking, they indicated that clan exogamy should be the pattern.

In former days when the whole village community of the Bharias consisted only of the same clan each male was related through blood to each female. Therefore, it is incestuous to marry within the village. There is, however, a change in the concept as multi-clan villages sprung up. In 1940s 18 informants had village exogamy whereas six reported having village endogamy. This is clearly in consonance with the type of multi-clan village prevailing in Patalkot valley. In 1970s the position, more or less, continued to be the same when 19 of the informants reported having practised village exogamy whereas two reported having practised village endogamy. The rest of the three who were unmarried stated that they had no objection to either type. Surprisingly the practice of village endogamy is on the decline whereas the incidence of village exogamy is on the increase. This phenomenon can be explained only with further probe which has not been attempted in this study.

An overall analysis of the social life of the Bharias of Patalkot valley indicates that the customs and manners relating to social life continue to be almost the same as in the former days. In other words, very little change is preceivable in the social life. Social life in terms of culture traits is considered as a core one and is not influenced much by external contacts.

Religious life

Three broad characteristics and well definable traits, namely, principal deity worshipped, services of the *Bhumka* at different ceremonies and disposal of the dead, have been analysed to find out the extent of persistence and change in the religious life of the Bharia tribe. A close scrutiny of the information available shows that as far as religious life is concerned there is absolutely no change.

Principal deity: Information about the principal deities of the Tribe, of the clan of the village, and of the family has been collected from the 24 sample informants. All of them informed that both in 1940s and in 1970s they consider *Baradeo* as their principal deity. Thus there is no change in the worship of the deity presiding over the Tribe.

As far as clan gods are concerned, all the informants agreed that neither they had any clan god in the past nor do they have the same at present.

Information on the different village gods worshipped by the Bharias is given in Table 15.

Table 15 shows the incidence of worship of different village gods as principal ones. It also shows that there is absolutely no change in the preference of the people so far as the village gods are concerned.

TABLE 15: **Incidence of village gods worshipped by the Bharias**

Village god	Worshipped in 1940s	Worshipped in 1970s
Bhimsen	24	24
Muthawa	11	11
Budidai	3	3
Hardal	2	2
Pandrimata	2	2
Matadai	1	1

Bhimsen continues to be the main village god for all the informants both in 1940s and in the 1970s. The concept about the next important village god varies from person to person. But all the same they maintain that there is no change in their belief. Thus *Muthawa*, *Budidai*, *Hardal*, *Pandrimata* and *Matadai* are considered the next important village gods for different people.

Principal family gods of the Bharia tribe vary from family to family. Sometimes they consider more than one god as the principal family deity. Table 16 gives the incidence of belief.

A perusal of Table 16 shows that different families have different family gods. Many families consider more than one god as their principal family deity. Altogether 17 family deities are reported to be worshipped by the informants. The incidence of worship continues to be the same as in 1940s.

To sum up, information regarding the principal deity worshipped by the Bharia shows that there is absolutely no change in their concept. This supports the hypothesis that religious belief, being a core culture trait, is not amenable to change owing to external contact.

Services of the Bhumka: Another religious trait, about which information is available, is the occasion when the services of the *Bhumka* (religious head) are availed of. Five occasions, about which answers, are available, are agricultural operations, constructure of a house, marriage ceremony, admission of outcastes and funeral.

TABLE 16: **Incidence of family gods worshipped by the Bharias.**

Family god	Worshipped in 1940s	Worshipped in 1970s
Budidai	7	7
Thakurdeo	9	9
Saklai	12	12
Dulhadeo	12	12
Dhanabai	12	12
Dhanthakur	12	12
Khodia	12	12
Khatarpal	13	13
Pahadia	22	22
Bhurabhagat	1	1
Bhavani	5	5
Mahadeo	3	3
Trishul	3	3
Narayandeo	2	2
Durga	3	3
Bhairavasani	2	2
Panch	2	2

In 1940s, 21 of the informants used the services of the *Bhumka* for the religious rites related to agricultural operations as against 20 in 1970s. For construction of a house 22 in 1940s and 21 in 1970s availed the services of the *Bhumka*. For marriage, for admitting an outcaste and for funeral ceremonies the views of the informants as to the role of the *Bhumka* remain the same as in 1940s. Thus, all sought the help of the *Bhumka* in admitting an outcaste, for funeral rites, and for marriage purposes. (The difference in the number reporting is because of the fact that some of the informants could not recollect the occasion.)

An analysis of the occasions when the services of the *Bhumka* were availed of shows that gradual change is perceptible in the case of secular occasions whereas no change is discernible in sacred occasions. With increased contact with outside, some of them view agricultural operations and construction of a dwelling unit as more secular than sacred. Marriage, admission of an outcaste and funeral continue to be considered as sacred occasions and as such no change is perceptible in them.

Disposal of the dead: Burial is the only method of disposal of the dead practised by the Bharias of Patalkot. Most of the Gonds outside the valley also practise burial. There appears to be no change in this practice to this day.

All the informants (save one) in 1940s and all of them in 1970s reported that they practised only burial in disposing of the dead. One of the 24 informants reported that cremation was practised in his family in 1940s, a view not conclusively substantiated on verification. It appears, therefore, that there is no change in this practice.

Leadership pattern

An attempt was made to assess the impact of external contact on the leadership pattern of the Bharias. The trait which is selected for this purpose is the medium dispensing justice in different contexts. The traditional Panchayat, the statutory Panchayat and the police authority are the three immediate institutions to look into the grievances of the people. The Statutory Panchayat is a new concept for the Bharia and it has been discussed elsewhere.

An analysis of the replies of the informants indicates that the traditional *Panchayat* weilds maximum influence even to this day.

In 1940s all the informants approached the traditional *Panchayat*, both in the case of infringement of the *lamjhana* contract and in cases of adultery or elopement. The position continues to be the same even to this day. In the case of personal hurt and theft 21 of them reported that they approached the traditional *Panchayat* in 1940s and the rest approached the police authority. As against this in 1970s, those reporting theft to the traditional *Panchayat* fell to 19 and personal hurt dropped to 15. The rest reported the matter to the police authorities.

This information reveals certain interesting phenomenon.

Infringement or grievance inflicted on those aspects which are more of social than of personal nature are reported mostly to the traditional Panchayat. In other words they continue to abide by the tradition oriented customs as far as the social values are concerned. Theft and personal hurt to them is more an infringement of personal rights and they feel that the proper authority to deal with it is the State administration. Therefore, the number reporting personal grievances to the traditional Panchayat is gradually decreasing and the number reporting the same to the police authority is steadily increasing. This can be attributed only to their change of attitude brought about by external contact, on the one hand, and the imbibing of new knowledge on the other.

REFERENCES AND NOTES

1. In almost all the cases the respondent Ego was head of the family. For checking up the veracity of information, particularly relating to 1940s, cross checks were made with elderly and knowledgeable members of the family.
2. The terms "earlier" and formerly" have been used to indicate 1940s and "now" and "today" to indicate 1970s.

7

THE DYNAMICS OF CHANGE

THE DYNAMICS of culture change, for long, has been the subject of interest to social scientists, particularly anthropologists. Change is part of the normal process of evolution. Hardly a generation in its attitudinal and normative behaviour is like its previous generation.

Culture is the outcome of interaction or the laws of inter-human behaviour. These are continually impinged upon and influenced by the physical and social environment. With the increase in the physical communications and consequent higher mobility of people, human behaviour is now influenced by a complex of factors. The culture and social changes occur at a much faster pace than ever before. Studies of people and their cultures the world over have brought out the fact that culture is dynamic. Its processes, trends or patterns depend upon various factors, more important among them being the ecological, physical and cultural forces which impinge upon the structural and institutional fabric of the recipient cultures.

Every change, in a way, brings in an element of cultural crisis and necessitates continuous adjustments. These are sometimes conscious efforts by the group as a whole to legitimise or rationalise a new behaviour and sometimes quiet and unnoticed. There had been a number of cases in which the community leadership has jointly decided to adopt a new behaviour and justified it in order to maintain cohesive group living or to curb the individual deviants. Whenever the community as a whole is threatened with disintegration as a result of individuals accepting a new behaviour or adopting a new practice, the group consciously decides to legitimise it. It is essentially a means for survival or existence. This contributes to the perpetuation of the traditional institutions and the social organisation. This behaviour is more apparant in the small, isolated and tradition-bound communities. In this connection, mention may be made of the practice of adopting the female child by the maternal uncle in certain communities. For some people which follow *Gotra* (lineage) exogamy, it is a socially sanctioned practice for the maternal uncle to adopt the female child so that she gets a new *Gotra*. This is generally done in cases where the parents fail to find a match for their daughter out of their *Gotra* but a suitable boy is available within the same *Gotra*. Again, it would be worth while to give an example of the practice of marriage by elopement, with the consent of the girl's parents. In certain tribal communities in India say, the Korkus of Madhya Pradesh, the bridegroom is permitted to elope with the bride in case the parents are too poor to afford an arranged marriage. This is generally done with the consent of the parents of both the bride and the bridegroom and the community leadership.

The above are just a few instances in which the community as a whole agrees to a new behaviour and legitimises it. Its outright rejection might have led to some open flouting of the community leadership.

As has been mentioned earlier, change is the result of physical as well as social forces. In this context, it may be mentioned, however, that contradictions in the very nature of human conditions, in general, are articulated with increasing sharpness in the development of the modern order.[1] Social change in India has been studied by many scholars and all of them have observed that the Indian society is flexible and dynamic like its counterparts in European countries and America.[2]

Social mobility in medieval India was closely linked with spatial mobility; availability of arable land alongwith other factors, such as floods, droughts, epidemics and stimulated migration.[3] Srinivas, quoting census reports, attributes these changes to new opportunities like educational, economic and political being caste free, helped in bringing about change.[4] Eisenstadt explains India's response to modernity in terms of "graduality of the impact of impinging cultures," and "dispersed effect" throughout the 18th, 19th and 20th centuries.[5]

Indian society is not homogeneous. Its broad canvas presents variegated groups of cultural scenes, and tribal culture is but one such group. Vidyarthi and Roy[6] analysed the broad spectrum of Indian tribal culture and pointed out that the factors responsible for transformation at the macro level can broadly be divided into two groups, "Traditional" and "Modern". The traditional process has brought about transformation in the secular, social and sacred spheres of the tribal culture through the regional "Hindu model". On the other hand the western, urban, industrial, developmental and democratic model, for induced change, was the result of the "modern" factor represented by the colonialists, the Christian missionaries and the different socio-economic developmental measures undertaken by the government. In addition, the growth of political consciousness also played a major part in the social change.[7] At the micro level, inter-tribal markets have also played a major part in bringing about both attitudinal and normative changes.[8] Various other authors[9] have also dealt with the subject in the Indian context.

In India, culture change has been studied by social scientists adopting different models or approaches. These were, by and large, based on the functional approach, followed by Majumdar, Naik, Dube, etc., the diffusion approach mainly adopted by Koppers, Fuches, Bose, etc., and finally the process of hyperculturation or the study of process of Sanskritisation, modernisation, etc. All these authors listed a number of factors based on their approach, methods and models of the study of change. However, the general picture that emerges out of all these discussions is that the dynamics of change is multi-factorial. These factors differ from place to place, from time to time and from situation to situation. Consequently, the effect, the response and the extent of change also vary from situation to situation and according to the temporal-spatial context. The change itself is never unidirectional.

In the present study of the Bharias of Patalkot, a little known community of Madhya Pradesh, some of the aforementioned concepts have been studied vis-a-vis the changing life of these people. This attempt, however, is basically related to the diffusion theory of culture change. It is a longitudinal study, making use of the case study method relying mainly on personal observation, and depth interviews and genealogical studies. The effort has mainly been to analyse and understand the "nature-man-spirit complex" of this rather obscure little community. In the process, the nature and extent of change taking place among the Bharias, the factors or forces responsible for such changes and the directions of change have been focussed upon.

Nature-man-spirit complex

The Bharias, by and large, live an isolated life. Their contact with the outside world is confined to the nearby markets where they do their shopping and occasionally to other villages where they go out for daily-wage labour. The steep hills around the Patalkot valley insulate them, to an extent, from the outside influences. As has been said earlier, the Bharia economy is more or less self-contained. They produce for self-consumption. It is essentially a consumers economy and the concepts of capital formation, investments, regeneration of wealth, etc., are just absent. The immediate environment around the valley provides them enough for their needs. The Bharias get their food supply from the forests, as also the timber and fuel wood. The fauna and flora take care of their many daily needs. The *mahua* flowers provide necessary ingredients for their alcoholic beverages, as also for food. The Dudhi river, cutting right across the valley, is an important source of water supply as also fish for food. Many important spirits and deities of the Bharias inhabit the forests and areas near the river.

It would be seen that the life of the Bharias and their economic activities are directly influenced by their immediate environment which not only provides for their daily needs but also keeps them away from outside influences. The whole lifecycle of the Bharias, in one way or the other, is the result of the interaction of man and environment. The mother earth provides food (grains, pulses and vegetables): the gods and goddesses that protect the life of the Bharias also live in the lap of the mother earth and after death, they are consigned to the mother earth. To the Bharias, the sacred of the sacreds is the mother earth, on which they live, on which they grow and in which they integrate after death. The quintessence of the Bharia philosophy is reflected in what may he termed as "Nature-Man-Spirit complex".

Nature and extent of change

The nature, extent and direction of change taking place among the Bharias of Patalkot have been discussed elsewhere in detail. For brevity the salient features are underscord here.

In order to have a more intimate perception of change, certain aspects of their culture, like material culture and economic life, social life, religious life and leadership were observed in detail by studying 24 sample families. It was revealed that changes were most perceptible in the material culture like dress and hair-styles of men and women, household articles, implements for economic activities and the like. There was also some perceptible change in the economic life of the Bharias. As regards social life, very little change was observed. Change in the religious life, however, had been almost negligible. The cultural lag thus was too apparent. The material culture meets the daily needs of the people and, therefore, a change occurs fast. The non-material culture is essentially a product of group living and descends down for generations. It is essentially a means for the survival of the group. A change in it may, in a way, threaten the structure of social institutions and values and ultimately affect the survival of the group itself. The leadership's authority is also jeopardised. The chain reaction of a change, as a matter of fact, acts as a barrier to new behaviour. The changes in non-material culture are, therefore, slow and imperceptible.

Society derives its strength from religion. As such, changes in the religious sphere are the last to occur. In fact both religion and society reinforce each other to survive.

Material culture is often considered at a peripheral culture trait; religious traits as core ones and social traits fall between the two.

In other words, culture traits which are considered peripheral were the most amenable to change. Those considered as core-culture traits experienced little or no change at all. The culture traits which fall in between showed both continuity and change.

Forces and agencies of change

The most important force of change in the case of the Bharias has been acculturation or, more specifically, hyperculturation. Though they live in comparative isolation, they do come in contact with their immediate neighbours, like the Gonds and the Hindus living around for ages. They also come in contact with the officials of the state, occasionally. But the single important contact is that of the weekly market at Chhindi which the Bharias visit very frequently. Though small in number some of the Bharias visited tehsil and district places taking back with them new ideas. Those who go in search of jobs outside the valley could also be considered as carriers of change. The peddlers making visits to the Patalkot valley, the school teacher and the political workers who visit the valley during elections to the legislatures also have had their share of contact with the Bharias of Patalkot. These external forces have made a considerable impact on the cultural life of the tribe.

Another force of change has been the State. The first of its kind affected the Bharias when the government banned shifting cultivation in 1954. This has necessitated a realignment of the balance of culture by adopting techniques, methods and means suitable to settled cultivation; as is natural, changes showed up first in the economic spheres. Agricultural implements and new techniques to suit settled cultivation were to be adopted, thus setting a chain-reaction in the cultural life of the Bharias.

Another wave of impact started when the Government decided to exploit the forest wealth of the valley by opening a fair-weather road. The contractors who were given the job of felling and transporting timber employed local labour. This resulted in the economic betterment of some of the Bharias on the one hand and contacts with the outsiders on the other.

Rate and direction of change

An attempt has been made to measure the rate of change taking place in the Bharia culture and its direction. The methods employed for this included, besides observation and general discussions with the people, ascertaining from the sample households the nature and characteristics of selected culture traits at two points of time (1940s and 1970s) by using genealogical techniques. This information provided a key to the rate of change taking place, in the community, in their various cultural aspects. The rate of change has been found to be much faster and intense in the case of material culture when compared to the social or religious aspects of life.

The example of change from the traditional male head-dress *Chindi* to that of *pagri,* used by the Gond and Hindu neighbours, can be cited in this respect. A beginning has also been made to use caps, a head-dress normally used by politically conscious people. Even a few of the Bharias, mostly of the younger generation, would not even use any head-dress, a practice among the Government officials and more modernised Gonds and Hindus. The same trend is discernible in the case of garments of the upper part of the body of men and women. A considerable number of males have changed over from *Bandi* to the modernised shirt being used by the outsiders. *Angia*, a traditional upper garment of women, is not used by anyone; instead more and more Bharia women use blouse, a modern upper garment worn by women outside Patalkot. The position about lower garments too indicates that the traditional style is being dispensed with and, as is natural, quicker by the younger generation irrespective of its utility under the environmental conditions. Material culture is influenced by the physical environment and the availability of resources. As such, by and large, it is utilitarian. However, people adopt a new dress, a new design for their house or a new type of headgear, even when it is not produced locally or does not suit the environment. It is basically the process of a community unconsciously adopting the life-styles of economically dominant groups or the process of hyper-culturation. This has, as already mentioned, been explained by various authors as Sanskritisation, modernisation, Khatrisation, etc.

Other aspects of material culture like utensils for cooking and serving food, carrying and storing water, agriculture implements, hunting implements, etc., also present, by and large, the same trend of change. More and more Bharias use house hold articles used by their neighbours.

The rate of change in the case of social and religious customs, on the other hand, has been slow and usually imperceptible. Social aspects tend to show signs of change whereas religious ones do not show any such sign. In this case, persistance is more common than change. Monogamy continues as the norm and the polygamy practitioners now tend to like monogamy, primarily due to economic reasons. The trend of change in the methods of acquiring spouses has been negligible. Arranged marriages persist though there is a slight drop in the incidence of practice. Marriage by service (*lamjhana*) continues as in 1940s. In the case of *bithalna* (widow remarriage) there is a definite change and none practise it, today.

Religious customs, on the other hand, persist as before. The worship of clan, family and village deities continues as before. The *Bhumka* (religious head) enjoys the same status and privileges as before, although a few of the educated Bharias now feel that in secular ceremonies like the construction of a house or starting of agricultural operations the *Bhumka* should not be bothered. In the disposal of the dead, marriages, admission of the outcasts, etc., the *Bhumka* enjoys the same status as he used to many decades back.

Factors accelerating or impeding change

Communication has been found to be the most important factor to accelerating change among the Bharias. The fair-weather road linking Tamia and Chhindi, plying of buses through this road, the fair-weather road constructed to transport timber from the valley, were all instrumental in increasing the tempo of change in the tribe. People from distant places were brought near the valley and people from the valley could extend their field of operation, thereby bringing about social intercourse between the Bharias and the outsider. Equally important was the role played by the Chindi market in bringing about change. To the Bharias it is more than an economic phenomenon. Besides selling commodities and buying merchandise it provides an opportunity for social interaction with people from all around. It is also a centre of social, religious and political activity of the tribes and castes of the region and accelerates change in the secular and religious values of the tribe. Thus the Chhindi market proved to be an important instrument of direct and indirect process of change.

Contact with officials particularly of the revenue department, forest department and police also provided impetus for change. Establishment of the primary school in Patalkot in early 1970 is yet another factor which tended to accelerate change among the Bharias, although it is too early to make an assessment.

On the other hand, the most outstanding factor impeding change in the life and culture of the Bharias of Patalkot is its geographical location. Situated in the valley about 400 feet deep surrounded on all sides by dense forest, the Bharias are physically insulated from the outside world. Before construction of some stone steps in 1953 in connection with the visit of the then President of India, outsiders seldom bothered to go down to the valley. Since then visits of outsiders has increased. These steps were, however, washed away within a couple of years of their construction, making a visit to Patalkot again a tedious and strenuous affair.

The other factor which stood in the way of culture change was the selectivity approach of the Bharias. They have been remarkably selective in the adoption of alien customs and culture traits. They have selected or assimilated, with suitable adaptations and modifications, such elements of alien culture as answered their needs and fitted them to their cultural life, rejecting others which were not compatible with their culture. The Bharias were very critical about the behaviour of petty officials who always tried to exploit them. This has left in them a kind of ambivalence towards the officials and as long as this attitude continues, government-sponsored activities cannot find whole-hearted support from the people. As, for example, the opening of the school did not evince much enthusiasm among the Bharias. They apprehended increased exploitation as they feared that the school building would be used more often by the visiting officials. Low attendance in the school is an indication of the attitude of the Bharias towards the educational institution as they hardly made any serious efforts to send their children to school. This is in addition to the reason stated earlier of their hesitancy to send their children to school because of their becoming earning membres of the family at an early age.

The general inertia of the Bharias towards progress and development and their preference for tradition too impedes change in their culture. This is evident from the fact that none of the Bharias have taken to advanced methods of agriculture like use of chemical fertilizers, improved varieties of agricultural seeds, irrigation systems or modern agricultural implements, although such facilities are offered to them by the community development authorities. Their neighbours, the Gonds, on the other hand have made use of such facilities.

Tribal welfare policy

The study does not provide sufficient data to suggest a policy for tribal welfare. However, some of the information which has gone into this study tend to indicate the importance of human factor in chalking out welfare programmes for tribal communities, particularly for those which are in the lower levels of development. In this case, the Bharias of patalkot have not taken the local officials, the promoters of economic development, into confidence. The reasons, as narrated by the people, are many. But the important one is the alleged exploitation by Government officials, which prompt them to keep the officials away. Consequently many of the benefits provided by the Government are not availed of. The study also indicates that success of a welfare programme largely depends on the receptivity of the people to accept it, which again depends on their desire for change. Agents of change have, therefore, a special role to play in instilling confidence among the people and thus generate desire for development and change.

Another point thrown up by this study is that "blanket programmes" at macro level do not often suit the local conditions and special groups. Programmes should, therefore, be formulated for "a people" and not for "the people"

REFERENCES AND NOTES

1. Eisenstadt, S.N., *Tradition, change and modernity*, Interscience Publications, New York, 1973, p. 7.
2. Srinivas explains that limitations of micro studies in India are too obvious which have great regional diversities, macro studies are likely to miss the nuances, refinements and subtelities. Srinivas, M. N., *Social Change in Modern India*, Allied Publishers, New Delhi, 1966, pp. 2.
3. Stein Burton, "Social Mobility and South Indian Hindu Sects", in *Social Mobility and Caste in India*, (Ed.) Silver Beg, J.
4. Srinivas, M.N.. op. cit. pp. 90.
5. Eisenstadt, S.N., op. cit. pp. 280-281.
6. Vidyarthi, L.P., and Rai, B. K., *The Tribal Culture of India*, Concept Publishing Co., Delhi, pp. 454-472.
7. Sachchidananda, *Profiles of Tribal Culture in Bihar*, Calcutta, pp. 149.
8. Sinha, D.P., *Culture Change in an Inter-Tribal Market*, Asia Publishing House, London, 1968.
9. These include: Dutta Majumdar, who explains contacts with, advanced cultures in his study of the Santhals; Robin Burling, in his study of the Garos, attributes imposition of external political control, new methods of agriculture and proselytising Christianity; Haimendorf who ascribes trade relations as the cause of change among Apa Tanis; Mandelbaum considered Hindus, British and Missionaries as agents of change among the Todas, the Kotas, the Badagas and the Kurumba of the Nilgiris; Ehrenfels attributed this change to the forest contractors and labourers, among the Kadars of Cochin. In his recent work, Aiyappan had found individual innovation, pride and prestige of the people and market places as the factors which had contributed to change among the Iravas of Mayur village in Kerala.

INDEX